Developing Strategies for International Business

Developing Strategies for International Business

The WRAP Process

J. Angus Gillon and Lynne Pearson

First published 2004 by
PALGRAVE MACMILLAN
Houndmills, Basingstoke, Hampshire RG21 6XS and
175 Fifth Avenue, New York, N. Y. 10010
Companies and representatives throughout the world

PALGRAVE MACMILLAN is the global academic imprint of the Palgrave Macmillan division of St. Martin's Press, LLC and of Palgrave Macmillan Ltd. Macmillan® is a registered trademark in the United States, United Kingdom and other countries. Palgrave is a registered trademark in the European Union and other countries.

ISBN 1–4039–3414–2

This book is printed on paper suitable for recycling and made from fully managed and sustained forest sources.

A catalogue record for this book is available from the British Library.

Library of Congress Cataloging-in-Publication Data
M/C Gillon, J. Angus, 1941–
    Developing strategies for international business : the WRAP process / J. Angus Gillon and Lynne Pearson.
        p. cm.
    Includes bibliographical references and index.
    ISBN 1–4039–3414–2
    1. Export marketing–Management. 2. International business enterprises–Management. 3. Strategic planning.
    I. Pearson, Lynne, 1965– II. Title.

HF1416.G545 2004
658.8'4–dc22   2004052093

10   9   8   7   6   5   4   3   2   1
13 12 11 10 09 08 07 06 05 04

Printed and bound in Great Britain by
Antony Rowe Ltd, Chippenham and Eastbourne

Contents

List of Figures

Foreword and Acknowledgments

The high tree of international trade has a long, strong and extremely convoluted root complex that has survived empires, despots, natural disasters, wars and seismic political and geological shifts over many millenia. While the tragic events of 9/11 in New York and Washington created a sharp intake of breath around the world and subsequent actions led to the turbulence that we see around us today, the globalization of business continues apace with new entrants competing with traditional firms and developing economies fast catching up with commercially maturing territories.

In this world it is no longer viable to retreat into a protected valhalla of domestic trade; the world is not so much on our doorstep as in our faces, and we need to find better ways of perceiving and dealing with it. That means meeting and addressing new challenges in ways that not only offer benefit and value but also provide frameworks within which commercial needs can be adapted to a variable range of cultural and market demands. Risk exists in all ventures, and in the complex planet that we inhabit it requires to be managed through foresight, awareness and intelligent judgment. Successful strategies, after all, can only be as effective as the people who implement them as well as those who develop them in the first place.

The contents of this book, and indeed the WRAP process itself, came together as a result of many years working with firms, and sometimes government bodies, to address the problems and opportunities that arise in doing business internationally. Creating order out of chaos may seem tough but creating real order out of perceived order presents a whole new challenge, and we responded to this need by linking information, rationale and judgment to the creative elements involved in developing successful strategies.

Essentially the book reflects a pragmatic approach to the world of global business in which prejudices and misconceptions can be recognized as constraints that need to be replaced by awareness and knowledge, and that gaining these attributes can be achieved within a reasonable timeframe, at least by those who seek them. We also know that the WRAP process works because many organizations that have had exposure to the total process or its individual elements now operate much more successfully in their international environment.

Our first set of acknowledgments must therefore go to all those directors, managers and officers who had the wit to learn, adapt, develop and apply the basic principles espoused, from whom we derived the confidence and dedication to continue the WRAP development. This book also contains many illuminating and sometimes cautionary tales and examples, each drawn from real situations and involving real people. Perfection in international strategy is rarely achieved and our focus is primarily concerned with the quality of the building blocks and the attributes of the other materials to be used in achieving appropriate objectives rather than the adoption of a grand architecture whose structural flaws become apparent as soon as the foundation stones are laid. At this developmental level, many mistakes are made and can be corrected or adjusted at the design stage. Our next set of acknowledgements therefore goes, along with our gratitude for helping us to enliven our readers' experience, to those whose follies and misapplied good intentions gave us many heart-stopping moments but also confirmed the validity of a better-informed approach.

The style and approach adopted in this book may be a consequence of combining American enthusiasm and Scottish guile. More likely, however, they derive from a shared dedication to building a strategic environment that can best enable companies to achieve their international aims, an enthusiasm for addressing the fresh challenges evident in the global marketplace, and a sense of humor which, although quirky, sustains us during the brain-banging sessions familiar to most strategists.

Special thanks go to Jackie Kippenberger, our commissioning editor at Palgrave Macmillan, for allowing us this opportunity and then leaving us alone to get on with it, to Jane Tulloch for de-confusing our computers on many angst-ridden occasions, and to Angus's wife Helen, who not only put up with some of the wierdest sleeping/waking schedules known to mankind but continued to provide encouragement all the way through the chapters.

1
International Business Rationale

Conducting business internationally has every appearance of becoming a more difficult and high risk proposition in a world environment that contains mistrust, misconception and misapprehension, and a fair amount of outright danger. Even in more stable times, a degree of political uncertainty may be paired with some level of economic instability across a range of territories worldwide. It is reasonable to assume that the only certainty is an essentially permanent state of flux in which businesses in domestic and international markets require an unprecedented degree of skill to maintain their balance.

This brings a complexity of operation in which priorities of supply, distribution, management time and corporate resource are often changing. Winning against known and unknown competition from companies, technologies, ideas and national preferences, and self imposed constraints, can be both risky and arduous. This requires strategies that take account of the factors involved, such as an objective supply of information, a means of rational prioritization, and a keen awareness of the cultural and motivational issues involved, within a framework that allows management to be effective over the entire context. To this end we have developed the WRAP process, which allows each of the elements to operate in conjunction with each other to provide the best opportunity to develop successful strategies in international markets.

Awareness counts

International business has existed for as long as there have been nations, and business between communities of various types existed long before that. It is also reasonable to suggest that apart from acts of God, natural disasters, wars, famines, imperialism and other inhibiting circumstances, the opportunity to conduct business and the volumes of business conducted have some co-existing relationship with the growth in communication possibilities, from the possession of common languages all the way through to the World Wide Web and email communication.

Nowadays, the evidence of the global extension of international business that has taken place can be seen not only in multinational operations like McDonalds, Pepsi Cola and Perrier, but also in the stock carried by retailers and distributors all around the world. Unless you are living in some extremely remote village in the upper Andes, or herding goats in one or two of China's western provinces, or living as a hermit or a monk, you will be in contact with an international commercial culture.

Great debates are currently in play about the nature of globalization and its impact, particularly on developing economies. There is significant substance in many of the issues raised that relate to such bodies as the World Trade Organization and the International Monetary Fund. However, it should be recognized that these debates are not about international business as such, but about the perceived skewing of the rules to favor some elements or regions against others, which is a form of economic imperialism that has become almost inextricably linked with fears of cultural domination.

Thus the 'Coca Cola' culture has become a symbol for many of a much wider ranging issue than simply the virtues of a particular fizzy drink. Balanced awareness of these issues, including the difference between economic or cultural imperialism and simply fulfilling market demand, should allow international business to proceed based on the merit of the case, product or price rather than allowing it to be co-opted by extremists of any persuasion.

Business is, in any event, essentially a simple thing. It was Dr Okhai, one of two Okhai brothers who became millionaires in the not so mean streets of Dundee and Fife, Scotland, who, when asked for the secret of their success, explained to a somewhat startled audience of sophisticated and knowledgeable financiers, business advisers and business people, 'We buy at a lower price. We sell at a higher price. Do you know a better way to make money?'.

That was thirty years ago, and it doesn't appear that things have changed much in the intervening years. The brothers imported packaging goods from the Indian subcontinent and sold them at premium rates, a practice which is often denigrated in the western economies, yet brought some jobs and some prosperity to Scotland. Should protectionism in the packaging business have been introduced, so that people in Scotland would be permitted to pay more for their packaging requirements? Many products enjoy some form of protection in their domestic markets, for reasons often related to local jobs and politics, yet many companies source products and components internationally, usually for reasons of lower cost or improved quality. Both these actions are part of international business and require to be addressed in dealing conceptually with domestic and foreign markets.

International thinking – negatives and positives

At the microeconomic level of individual corporate decision making, it is helpful to at least be aware of these global issues. Even more useful is awareness of the key current domestic issues in the territories to be addressed, as political and economic trends can affect not only market prices, volumes of business available, competitive strategies and quality requirements, for example, but also determine whether or not the desired business is accomplished at all.

Extending a business successfully beyond domestic borders can provide great benefits; there are also some downside risks that can ensnare the unaware and minimize, rather than maximize, returns. The point of doing business internationally is to enhance and improve profitability and competitive advantage. In order to be taken seriously in the territories to be addressed, it is helpful to show at least some awareness of the commercial culture and environment. Even though the marketing plan may involve recruiting a local distributor or agent, who may be accustomed to the relative ignorance demonstrated by his or her prospective principals, it is surprising how much more focused the distributor can become, and how much improvement can be seen in corporate sales, when his or her country is treated with the respect that a little awareness can bring.

We had a US based client that operated its European office from a small town in southern England. The products supplied were capital goods of a highly technical nature and a plan was devised to extend sales from the UK, where they were entirely located, to Germany, Italy, France and Spain. The drawback was that the plan also envisaged these new European sales being developed by sending members of the UK sales force to each of these continental territories to make new contacts and bring in business. This plan may have worked better had any of them been able to converse in technical jargon in German, Italian, French or Spanish, but the company was convinced that technical staff within the target companies would be able and willing to speak English fluently and comfortably.

Fortunately for the company, this particular plan came to an end quite rapidly when the company took a stand at a major exhibition in Düsseldorf, Germany, and hired a local English teacher as a translator. It became evident within the first day or so that German engineers and buyers did indeed prefer to speak German when discussing complex technical requirements, and that English teachers were not ideally suited to the translation of technical terminology. Furthermore the company's UK sales force, in heavy attendance, was pretty well cut off from their sales prospects by this language barrier.

A new plan was rapidly devised that included local distributors, and the company proceeded from there to a somewhat more successful sales campaign in continental Europe. The main lesson to be learned from this tale is a simple one: lack of awareness is likely to lead to expensive errors and that revelation of such ignorance to prospective buyers can cost the company much time, expense and effort in repairing the initial damaging impression. Figure 1.1 identifies some personal traits that we suggest should be overcome before becoming involved in international business. A frame of mind that is suitably receptive to dynamic change and unfamiliar situations is not a 'useful buy/optional extra' in non-domestic markets. It is, in fact, a prerequisite for developing a successful international business.

Figure 1.1 Seven Traits That Should be Overcome Before Attempting International Business

---

1. A strong and deeply rooted desire not to travel abroad.
2. A strong desire to alter other people's lifestyles and cultures to suit the needs of your particular product, service, or traditional way of doing business.
3. Lack of basic cultural awareness, which may be taken as a mark of disinterest or disrespect.
4. Dismay regarding the need for communication in a foreign language.
5. Suspicion of foreign attitudes or behavior, whether on the grounds of war participation or non-participation, perceived corruption, personal prejudice, conviction that foreigners have always been out to get you, and sundry other complaints.
6. An assumption that other territories offer less competitive markets, higher pricing and profitability, and require less effort to get them.
7. Inability to recognize and learn from your mistakes.

In more visionary terms, international business provides an opportunity to extend product sales, increase profitability, develop new sources of supply and create international presence and branding. Achieving this requires awareness, solid management effort and well planned utilization of company resources. Figure 1.2 outlines some of the gains to be made in going along this road.

Figure 1.2 Eight Potential Benefits of International Business

1. Significant extension of existing market(s).
2. Exposure to fresh opportunities and alternative cultures, bringing greater breadth of vision.
3. Wider access to sources of supply.
4. Access to wider opportunities in mergers, acquisitions, joint ventures and partnerships.
5. New product possibilities in meeting new market demand.
6. Opportunity to develop worldwide presence and branding.
7. Increased competitive edge through ability to cross-feed supply and sourcing.
8. Potentially greater profitability.

In many cases, companies are able to create their own odds in achieving success. The world may not be fair, but in general terms the business culture is agnostic: that is, companies with an established presence in the international dimension will have an accrued reputation built up over years of developing relationships in a wide range of territories that is at least sufficiently strong to keep them in business, while for relatively new or smaller entrants the business world will view developments with interest.

The essential rationale

The essential rationale for becoming seriously involved in international business is that, for most of us, we are already in it. Most of the products that we live with on a day to day basis have some kind of international component, whether we are talking about food, cars, leisure pursuits or furnishings. It is therefore in our interests to ensure that our companies also gain the benefit of a world market for supply and sourcing. Figure 1.3 shows the relative size of key world economies in 2001, in which one of the most interesting features is that the combined economies of a few South East Asia countries was larger than that of China, and the combined European Union economic area was larger than that of the USA. Depending on the perspective, the shape and potential of world markets can vary dramatically.

It may be helpful to consider that no matter which market we regard as our own domestic market, the rest of the world offers a far larger

Figure 1.3 Comparative Economies Expressed as Gross Domestic Product (US$ 000 billions) 2001

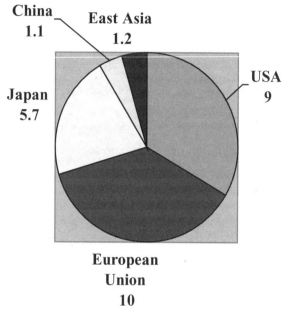

China 1.1 — East Asia 1.2

Japan 5.7

USA 9

European Union 10

Note: East Asia includes South Korea, Taiwan, Singapore and Hong Kong.
Source: National Governments

field in which our products and services may be sold or sourced. With around 300 countries in the world, and many of these possessing significant regional markets internally, the choice of targets is wide.

Nevertheless, addressing non domestic markets also provides a significant challenge as many constraints are imposed both within the countries approached and within the managerial consciousness of the supplier. Some can be easily surmounted by adopting a rational approach, while others require both detailed information and a broad understanding of such issues as business culture and relationship development. Figure 1.4 outlines some of the more common issues that are likely to require serious consideration in order to compete successfully in the international forum.

The common thread running through all these potential downside risks is one of attrition. If poorly planned, the process of developing an international presence can drain money, effort, and focus from the business and weaken its overall financial position with little contribution to the bottom line. The implication is straightforward: inter-

Figure 1.4 Ten Constraints on International Business

1. Potential disorientation of product or service focus in the process of market expansion.
2. Downside options in currency exchange rates.
3. Higher risk in addressing unfamiliar markets.
4. Higher risk in addressing new product, service or supply sources.
5. Poor resource allocation between domestic and international business.
6. Added costs in travel, management and business development.
7. Poor or confused market prioritization and international product or service vision.
8. Time and resource absorbed in developing significant presence.
9. Foreign competitor response, both overseas and domestic.
10. Difficulties in developing effective distribution networks and supply chains

national markets will not take care of themselves. They require active management, and management that needs to be built on an ability to grasp complex problems and a willingness of take decisions and follow through on them.

Exporting v. international business

International business is manifested in its essential form as the import–export trade carried on daily by companies of all sizes around the world. At its most basic this is perceived as a relatively simple exchange, in which foreign customers place orders for goods or services that are subsequently delivered with the appropriate paperwork intact. In many instances the concept is extended to embrace the foreign distributor or agent, who takes on responsibility for marketing and sales in a given territory in return for an agreed percentage of sales revenues or substantially discounted product purchases. At this stage it is common for manufacturing, R&D, logistics, and promotional activities to be concentrated entirely in the domestic market, and to be focused primarily on serving that market in the first instance. This provides a basic description of the way in which many businesses approach international markets.

In this incarnation the export process tends to be driven by opportunism: the chance to make contact with a potential new customer in Brazil one week, and to fill an order from Malaysia the next. It may all work perfectly well, as far as it goes, and quite possibly show a profit. But how far does this approach actually take the business in the longer term?

Consider the limitations. Seizing and diligently pursuing leads wherever in the world they arise provides little opportunity for developing expertise and building substantial presence in a local market, nor does it allow sufficient concentration of effort to address market specific demand. It also commits the management to significant time and expense in allocating equivalent resources to each territory, regardless of the potential returns expected from that market. Taken to its extreme, it results in the business spreading itself so thinly around the globe that there is little prospect of building up the financial or developmental momentum to compete effectively in what are, after all, other people's domestic markets.

This simple method of organizing sales in non domestic markets begs a multitude of questions. What constitutes a realistic expectation of market performance and, by extension, business success? How can the company assess whether its performance is in line with these expectations? What is likely to be gained (or lost) by entering a given market? What level of resources, both financial and managerial, can and should be committed to achieving objectives in a given market? Most importantly, how can these objectives be reasonably defined in the first place? And behind these questions lie deeper issues of long term customer focus, competitive positioning, supply chain relationships, and manufacturing or service delivery in international markets.

It is often regarded as a truism that international business is driven by 'opportunism', by which is generally meant the ability and willingness to seize and exploit new business opportunities at short notice on a wider scale. In practice, opportunities do not simply spring into existence and wait to be recognized: they need to be identified, assessed, and brought to fruition through careful and active management, which can most effectively be brought to bear through its responsiveness to the organization's overall strategic focus.

Figure 1.5 demonstrates the potential for losing focus in a world in which options need to be assessed and decisions taken even as circumstances themselves are changing. It's easy to take the decision that there's no point in upsetting the applecart when sales are in fact being made, but this potentially leaves the company at the mercy of distributors or other agents with their own strategies and agendas. In international as in domestic business, you only control your returns if you control the strategic basis for developing business.

In our view, it is now essential to move away from the export driven business rationale to embrace the wider concept of international business as a systematic activity with a defined strategic focus that encompasses not just sales, but decisions about sourcing, supply, and

Figure 1.5 Brazil is Bigger Than Peru. Honest

'Best market equals best distributor' is a concept commonly found on websites and in the promotional literature of firms with an interest in foreign markets: Distributors in fifty countries. Or a hundred countries, or possibly even more. It may work well, or it may lead to an expensive confusion of priorities. Consider an example.

Company X is a UK based supplier of manufacturing equipment which is sold primarily through distributors in over 100 countries around the world, ranging from key industrial economies such as the USA to rapidly developing markets in South and East Asia. For some time, one of its primary concerns had been the prioritization of markets in Latin America. Given the sheer size of the region, sales seemed unaccountably low, but this very problem of size also demanded that order be brought to resource allocation across the territories in order to ensure its most effective application.

'Our best market in the region right now is Peru,' said the MD. 'The distributor there sells far more than in any other country.' Peru, so the assumption went, represented the largest unit volume of sales by territory, which therefore made it the key Latin American market and a high priority in terms of management time and support.

Was this really the case? An assessment of the customer industry base in a range of the larger Latin American countries revealed that Brazil, Mexico, and Argentina were potentially vast markets for the company's equipment, particularly when compared to Peru. Yes, both foreign and domestic competitors were present and active in each country, but that was essentially down to the fact that there existed sizeable and growing markets worth competing for.

It also suggested that, as the distributors in these countries were regularly outperformed by their colleagues in Peru, rapid remedial action was required to target and achieve a credible market share. Brazil quickly emerged as the priority market, and a change of distributor, accompanied by clear awareness of the commercial objectives to be attained in the market, began to earn Company X the financial returns it hadn't previously expected from this territory.

And Peru? It was highly unlikely that extra resourcing could have improved performance in this market, which was in fact just about as good as it could be. It continues to turn over quietly, at a low but steady rate, just as it should do.

production, and which sees the domestic market as an integrated aspect of a larger, worldwide marketplace.

International business also implies a commitment to utilizing international markets as a platform for developing and strengthening the overall financial and market position of the firm. It posits a developed awareness of competitive activity in a range of markets, and an ability to build on this awareness to identify new ways of gaining or enhancing competitive advantage in a world that will never, whatever else happens, remain static.

Isn't this really a matter of semantics, you might ask, or just a different way of thinking about the situation? Exactly: it's an entirely different way of thinking about the problems and opportunities thrown up by engagement with the rest of the world. It is a commitment to viewing the world in all its variety as an opportunity rather than as a threat, or as a separate civilization to be kept entirely at arms' length while endeavoring to profit from it. It's about engaging with the world constructively.

Constructive engagement sounds very basic, but it possesses two prerequisites that are in practice far more complex than this simple phrase would suggest. It requires *information*, which entails a clear awareness of the actual conditions obtaining in relevant territories and an ability to make objective comparisons between markets. At the same time, it's clear that no amount of information can ever be absolutely comprehensive or indisputably accurate in every particular. Making sense of these anomalies requires *judgment*, the ability to comprehend what the information is actually telling us and make decisions on that basis.

Pulling it together: the international mindset

As we will demonstrate in succeeding chapters, successful international business practice requires both hard information and flexible judgment. However, the primary criterion indicating a real ability to operate in global markets is an even 'softer' issue, difficult to define succinctly but nevertheless of absolutely crucial importance. It is what we shall call an *international mindset*.

An immense amount of research, consultancy, and business publishing has been dedicated to analyzing the cultural issues that become so crucial in managing multinational operations, and this area of research provides much of the current thought leadership in the field of international business. However, before an individual arrives at the stage of managing any aspect of a transnational corporation it is useful to examine some ways of thinking about the world that encourage adaptability and provide a mental framework for identifying and building on business opportunities in diverse cultural circumstances.

Tolerance. No matter how open minded an individual may believe themselves to be, it's certain that exposure to unfamiliar cultures and business practices will sooner or later bring them into contact with situations and modes of behavior that they find it difficult to deal with, or indeed positively dislike. The good news is that it is not necessary to like them. It is simply necessary to work within the system, and accept that the system works the way it does. This also presupposes that the individual will be actively willing to learn about the business and cultural habits of new customers and will refrain from randomly imposing his or her own values on the situation.

Mental flexibility. International business is not just a matter of becoming accustomed to jet lag, or to superficially different modes of behavior. It's likely that many of the people you meet will have somewhat different ways of thinking about the world, and will approach such issues as problem solving and negotiation from a new angle. It is well worth trying to get inside the minds of your customers and business partners and endeavor to understand *how* and *why* they think the way they do. Only in this way can you really build up a relationship that is not dogged by mutual incomprehension and misunderstanding, and only in this way can you truly get the most out of the business you're pursuing.

These issues and others related to them will be explored more thoroughly in Chapter 4, in which we deal with international business cultures. However, arming yourself with an appropriate approach from the outset will make the process of international strategic development easier and much more fruitful.

Figure 1.6 Summary of Key Points

- Most people are already in contact with international commercial culture
- It is helpful to develop awareness of current global issues, as well as of international commercial concerns
- International business provides opportunities to extend product sales, increase profitability, develop new sources of supply, and create international presence and branding
- Potential gains include significant expansion of existing markets, exposure to fresh opportunities, and increased competition edge and profitability
- A mindset receptive to change and unfamiliar situations is a prerequisite for success in international business
- International business has wider implications than opportunistic exporting

2

Overview of the WRAP Process

Sun Tzu was a famous Chinese leader, general, advisor or possibly something else, depending on whose historical interpretations you accept. There is also the possibility that he was several people (spanning many hundreds of years, but quoted as a single entity) whose musings and observations on the subject of military strategy were directed not at describing the minutiae of military engagements, but towards the broad sweep of strategic actions. These actions can be readily translated into modern competitive situations. In the time of Sun Tzu, competition largely took the form of armed conflict, and his maxims consequently reflect the necessities of battle; nevertheless, many can be easily transposed. Do not engage the enemy on unfavorable terrain. Do not pit the weakest of your forces against the strongest of the enemy's forces. Simple and obvious in many ways, these concepts could have borne much more repetition during the many subsequent centuries of military blunders.

While the applications of Sun Tzu's thoughts, as described in *The Art of War*, to management practice are many and varied, certain observations on strategy development and deployment are particularly relevant. First of all, it is critical to gain at least some awareness of the external circumstances in which the organization intends to operate. The relative strength of the competition, the nature of the market, and all the other issues will make a critical contribution to eventual success or failure, and it therefore makes sense to learn something about them so that their attributes can be used positively to develop strategic aims.

It is equally important to make an honest assessment of a firm's internal circumstances. These include not only capabilities and resources, but also the ultimate corporate strategic objectives, and will determine in large part where and how to strike in order to obtain

Figure 2.1   The Benefits of Learning, or How to Achieve Success Quicker and Better

A small biotech firm based in Britain had everything going for it. The company was focused on biotechnology for plants, and distributed throughout the UK a disease limiting product manufactured in the US. Subsequently it decided to expand by exporting to continental Europe, in particular to the Netherlands, where the huge horticultural industry appeared to be a natural target. There seemed to be no competition, and the country is within 50 miles of the UK. Nevertheless, sales were negligible.

Let's try Sun Tzu. Be aware of the terrain, or nature of the market. There is a regulatory process in existence, even for plant biotech products, in all developed territories. This product had approvals from UK laboratories, and the company assumed, somewhat imperially, that UK approvals allowed access to the rest of the world. The potential Dutch customers, however, were not about to risk their livelihood and lifestyle on the say-so of a foreign laboratory, and would not buy until their domestic laboratories gave the product a proper Dutch approval.

The other issue is the competition. Know your enemy, or words to that effect, says Sun Tzu. Of course there was competition, from every other natural and chemical product used to keep the industry thriving over many decades. The competition did not just encompass biotech products. This analysis seems simple, and it is simple, but a modicum of awareness linked to a little bit of thinking things through often seems uncommonly rare!

victory, aka success. It is also crucial to understand how to manage the relationship between external and internal circumstances in order to bring about the desired outcomes.

At the distance of three millennia from Sun Tzu's time, this description of strategic thinking is one that can be fully endorsed as a succinct description of the key elements of strategy development woven into a closely-knit plan for action. It has particular relevance in the realm of corporate strategy development in a global marketplace, where the stakes are high and the choices at hand are almost without limit.

Look at the problem in its practical manifestation. Various people, at various times, can be found promoting the virtues of established markets, developing markets, small high-growth markets, or geographically remote markets from Bolivia to Tadzhikstan. So which markets truly offer realistic and promising business development prospects, and which are just more trouble than they're worth? Involvement in foreign markets costs money, requires management time and skill, and demands energy and commitment, but how much of this investment is sensible and how much is simply irrecoverable money down a hole? As with advertising and political policy-making, poorly costed budgets tend to lead to poor returns.

Then there's also the ultimate litmus test of almost all business development programs: they need to provide a satisfactory return, but in many cases it is questionable whether the 'satisfactory' return is feasible or takes into account other benefits and advantages of competing in foreign countries. Finally, hammering out the solutions to these problems can potentially be a long-winded process, and by the time it's completed the landscape may have changed, rendering the whole exercise ultimately useless.

The primary difficulties with developing any kind of coherent strategy for global markets is the challenge of identifying, reviewing, and establishing genuinely strong business prospects, rather than drifting randomly from one opportunity to another. Many firms prefer to find and pursue a series of single, randomly occurring opportunities without considering their place or value in the overall strategic framework. Such 'opportunity-hopping' often occurs because managers are, or perceive themselves to be, required to produce returns quickly in foreign markets, usually on the basis of budgets that are constantly under pressure from domestic requirements. Under these circumstances, stepping back to take a considered view of international markets and their true value to the company may look like an unnecessary luxury. As long as the potential leads keep coming, they are pursued without reference to strategic worth or priority. Opportunism is a fine, well-established entrepreneurial practice; opportunism without a framework of reference, however, can lead to high risk and wasted resources.

What is WRAP?

WRAP (World Rational Analytical Prioritization) evolved as a rational response to increasingly complex and sometimes confused briefings from consultancy clients, who often sought to address whole rafts of international strategy issues without consistent awareness of the context in which they are located. It became evident that in order to achieve (and sometimes to create) global corporate objectives, it was essential to develop a framework within which the various issues could be evaluated, reviewed and prioritized and strategies properly focused on achievement in a competitive environment. This approach also allows the company to build up and hold expertise in identifiable key markets, permits the full exploitation of business opportunities and, in the longer term, offers a prospect of enhanced profitability that can help drive the company further along the path to global expansion.

The process, in its full development, comprises a series of steps in which focus, information and prioritization are critical stages in formulating strategies. The process can also be broken down into component parts and used as required to review established strategies and priorities on a rational and objective basis, and even to help determine the rationale behind competitor strategies. Figure 2.2 shows the WRAP process as it is conceptualized, and while it is reasonable to assume that firms dealing in international business already have knowledge and awareness of some elements, experience indicates that with some notable exceptions (not always major corporations) the content of each step is often flawed or inadequate.

WRAP works by building a series of 'capital' units (steps) in which each element combines with other elements to add value to the overall process. In creating a strategy, its worth is measured by its effectiveness in implementing and achieving agreed corporate objectives; equally, the viability or attainability of these objectives is assessed and evaluated during the development of the WRAP process, as each element is implemented. For example, if an objective is to cut a three meter length of string from a roll, it will be identified quite early on in the process if the roll itself is only two meters long. A four-meter length may allow the objective to be achieved but again, only if the cutting implement is sharp enough. Additionally, there is a requirement for a measuring capability, somebody or something available to do the deed, and the will to actually make the cut. All these elements combine to create the achievement of the objective and understanding the elements involved in cutting string or implementing international strategy adds value to the entire process. The value that is added is the ability to adjust or

Figure 2.2 The WRAP Stairway

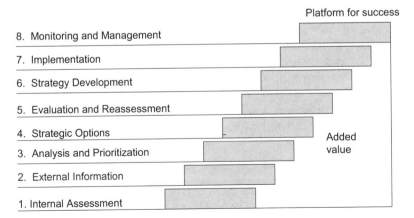

amend strategies and objectives in the light of changing circumstance or preferences without the need to start the whole process all over again.

Figure 2.3 indicates a better known WRAP interpretation that exhibits some of the more common aspects of strategy development based on inadequate information and poor focus on unrealistic objectives, leading to indistinct prioritization and a consequently skewed strategy. Most companies possess some information relevant to each step, either formally or informally, but much of it is based on assumption, pieces of information fed back from distributors and others in the market, and subjective preferences. This doesn't mean that the strategies adopted won't work at all, but they are unlikely to maximize opportunity and focus scarce resources where they will bring most corporate benefit.

Figure 2.3 A Typical Un-WRAPped Stairway

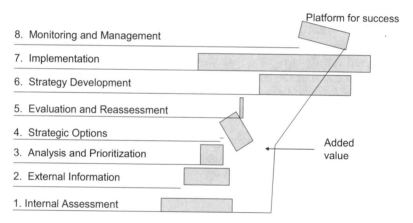

The elements involved in the WRAP process are not unique or unknown, but their application in a rational and comprehensive framework adds far more value to corporate strategy-building than a patchy or irregular acquisition of information and development of options. Put simply, it is derived from the school of thought espoused by Drucker and others that a rational, information-led approach to management issues generally works better and more effectively than one based on hunch and hope.

How does WRAP work?

The WRAP process (Figure 2.2) as described proceeds in eight steps, each of which is made up of several components that address essential

Figure 2.4   The WRAP Process

One fine day a man came riding out of the American west. Not just a lonesome cowboy, but a senior executive vice-president of one of the world's largest engineering contractors focused at that time on mechanical construction mainly in the oil and gas sectors. His brief was to identify and exploit an alternative industry sector in which his company's skills and resources could be successfully and competitively applied on an international scale.

His first action was to buy in and examine a large map of the world. His next, wisely, was to call in consultancy help. The problem he faced, starting from ground zero, was difficult but his approach would break even better men than he. He had effectively no information on the wide range of sectors outside oil and gas that utilized mechanical construction (agriculture to rock shows) and no information on the hundreds of countries around the world outside the US. He had no way of prioritizing sectors or countries, and no criteria to help establish priorities other than 'mechanical construction', 'accessible' and 'international'. His original plan was to look at the world, determine which relevant sectors were growing, and work out a world market development strategy.

Patently, the first requirement was to introduce focus to this exercise, and this was achieved by taking his simple criteria and adding a further qualification called 'consistent with the corporate culture'. That is, let's exclude rock shows and other industries where the market is fragmented, and let's specifically review industries where the international customer base is confined to a relatively small number of extremely large organizations, thus equating with overall corporate experience. Ultimately, the consultants came up with the defense industry as a potentially explosive sector for the company! The Mediterranean Basin was chosen to test this analysis, because it was easily accessible, mostly friendly, and contained a significant number of both American and domestic military bases, and a few selected countries in the region were targeted as potential customers. These were prioritized through further market research that identified opportunity, competition and budgets, as well as routes to market and critical product issues.

There was now information- and analysis-based industry and territorial focus, and strategies were developed to access the priority markets, including adjustment in the agency structure to take account of the fact that strengths in the defense sector, rather than oil and gas, were now required. The exercise was successful, and the company extended the adopted strategies to this market worldwide, under the direction of a new Directorate. Over the ensuing years several billions of US dollars were generated in the sector, and the man from the West returned home with a substantial bonus package to an extremely comfortable retirement...

aspects of international strategy development. Each component is designed to stimulate consideration of a range of critical issues, while at the same time highlighting and clarifying the relationships between different parts of the strategy program. In this way, WRAP provides the tools enabling successful mapping and navigation of both the known and the uncharted territories of international business.

The first series of steps involve the development of both internal and external information, on a rational basis, as a means of bringing focus to the project. In the second series of steps the process requires the analysis of the data and information to indicate strategic priorities and thus provide a solid foundation for the formulation of strategic options. The third series encompasses strategy development, which, critically, also includes laying plans for the implementation and monitoring of the longer-term strategic program.

Is the process complex? Yes, in the sense that it requires thought, attention, hard work and good judgment at every stage if the final strategy is to be successful. No, in the sense that WRAP breaks the process of strategy definition into discrete components capable of being addressed systematically and cross-referenced against one another to promote a robust and realistic outcome.

Step 1: Internal assessment

The initial step in the process is an internal assessment of key aspects of the organization's existing resources and capabilities. This critical assessment operates as a foundation for all of the decisions and actions that follow from the strategy development process, as it defines what the organization is capable of doing and willing to do, and helps determine what it needs to achieve in order to make the pursuit of business in global markets worthwhile. This in turn is crucial to the company's ability to set objectives that are both attainable and profitable.

The internal assessment takes into account five categories of information as a means of defining the framework within which the organization currently operates. These include:-

- the resources available to the company for the development of new business while maintaining current activities. This encompasses not just the obvious issue of financial resources, but also takes into account those of a managerial and technical nature, as well as any existing international infrastructure that might contribute to further global development.
- the existing line of products and/or services, including the range of products, costs and pricing, current profitability, and any R&D pipeline.
- the type of customers who currently buy the organization's products or services. This will assess the present range and segmentation of the customer base, its geographic range, and the sector trends and drivers that impact upon the medium- to long-term availability of the customers.

- background to the geographic markets in which the company currently has a presence, or has declined or failed to develop one. This covers any existing sales and service infrastructure, market positioning and awareness, competitive assessment of the marketplace, as well as the shape of the current supply chain.
- the culture which exists within any firm or corporation. For example, in firms operating within the defense industry, executive personnel are often drawn from military sources and the company is structured to relate to procurement practices in a department of defense environment. Such firms find it difficult to adapt their management and thought processes to differently structured environments, such as more free-flowing business cultures in which procurement processes and management styles are more flexible.

Step 2: Development of external information

The second step in this phase of the WRAP process comprises two interlocking fixtures. These are:-

- the establishment of parameters and criteria
- the collection and matching of information that relates specifically to the agreed parameters and criteria, although contextual information may provide further help in analysis

This step is more fully covered in Chapter 5, but essentially parameters can be defined as the geographic or technical scope to be addressed in information gathering, and criteria are those key issues that companies use to determine market prioritise. Proper focus will lead to an ability to prioritize market potential in terms of corporate objectives and requirements, in some cases quantitatively and in others as quality markers.

Step 3: Analysis and prioritization

Based on analysis of the results of internal assessment and information gathering, priorities can be established that focus the strategy both geographically and in relation to the criteria. In essence, the market or location (national or regional) that matches most closely the criteria would become the number one priority target market. Getting there, however, is not quite so simple, when it is considered that the matches that are being sought may be required to conform, typically, to up to six criteria (both quantitative and qualitative), and demand cross-comparison in up to forty or fifty countries worldwide. While it may be feasible to match and cross-compare such volumes of information manually, we find it easier and quicker to build a simple computer model incorporating quantitative data, convert amenable qualitative information into quantitative rankings, and use the remaining qualitative information as qualifying factors.

For example, an American or Japanese company seeking to refocus its strategic efforts might select a regional parameter such as 'western Europe' extending to the accession territories (Poland, Czech Republic, Hungary, Baltic States, and so on) and its research criteria might include, in the company's industry sector:-

- market size
- market growth
- product pricing
- key international competitor presence
- presence of domestic industry
- amenability to import.

This information requires to be gathered for each country, of which there are over 30, and information relating to each criteria, for each country, requires to be compared with every other country in order to determine priority target markets and rank countries accordingly. The application of some knowledge and judgment in this exercise, such as recognizing that most markets in Latvia are likely to be smaller than most markets in Germany, is a useful tool in addition to the computer model, so that the matrices can be simplified and grouped. Complex as it sounds, this process can actually achieve results quite quickly when compared with traditional market research methodologies, simply by focusing exclusively on the criteria identified above. This is covered more fully in Chapter 7.

Step 4: Determining strategic options

At this stage, further research into determining routes to market, legal niceties and other issues can be undertaken. This additional information will be used to determine what options are available in addressing the target markets or locations, and may be valuable in comparing current corporate activities with preferred approaches. It is not unknown, indeed it is fairly common for companies to spend many years developing markets without ever maximizing their potential, which is often constrained by such factors as the product strategies pursued by local distributors and the willingness of companies to settle for an unambitious market share.

So what are strategic options? Well, at least 5 key issues require to be addressed during this step. These can be identified as:-

- routes to market, including product support where appropriate
- range and design of products and services to be sold, and pricing strategies to be adopted
- management requirements
- acquisition, joint venture and other possible partnerships
- hard elements such as tariff barriers, logistics, packaging and language, and international communications

Each issue requires careful review and discussion, although the range of aspects to be covered will vary with each company. For example, a German firm that has identified China as its primary target market in Asia may prefer to use existing offices in Australia to manage developments in China, as it is closer to the market. On the other hand, if the company's intention is also to manufacture components or products in China, would that not be a better base for management, even if there is an implication that a new management team may be required? Or would it be better and easier, given China's legal, commercial and business cultures, to simply sub-contract to a Chinese partner, which would limit involvement to investment and some measure of quality control? Each of these options can be illuminated and broadly evaluated both in terms of cost and resource requirements as well as market potential, using the information gathered earlier in the WRAP process. Without that information, determining the most appropriate options becomes entirely a matter of guesswork or probabilities based on information and guidance gleaned from others with some experience of the market; such sources can be invaluable, but their value should be in informing and enlightening, not in determining the course of corporate strategy. This is covered in more detail in Chapter 9.

Evaluation and reassessment

At this stage companies have the opportunity to re-evaluate their current positioning and corporate objectives, which can be radically altered as a result of new strategic options and opportunities that may be available to them. I know of one CEO who admitted that he was comfortable with selling a few of his products in each of many countries worldwide; with the benefit of the kind of information available through the WRAP process, and a little extra effort on his firm's part, he was able to focus primarily on those territories that offered the opportunity to maximize his product sales with little discernable effect on sales in non-priority territories. That way, his corporation makes more money and is better able to compete internationally.

Strategy development

There are many books published on types of international strategy that can be, or have been adopted and implemented. The strategies outlined range from off-the-wall creative concepts to the very simplest regimes, and it is not our intention to review the nature and scope of each possible strategy that could be implemented. The critical strategic element in the WRAP process is that strategic objectives should be guided by information and awareness, from which will evolve strategies appropriate to each circumstance. It is not necessary to adopt a single strategy for global implementation, although such formula-driven approaches sometimes work well in the consumer industries. It is also unnecessary to attempt to create individual strategies for each territory, as many countries show sufficient similarity of structure to allow a more formulaic approach. We are back to the old yet extremely useful concept, use your brain to ally information and imagination.

The key characteristics of strategic development espoused in the WRAP process can be encapsulated as:-

- understand corporate objectives; they are more specific than a mission statement
- research information and data that is relevant to the organization's products or services
- focus on priorities, both territorial and product
- evaluate the opportunity
- use both the information developed and awareness of the business and cultural environments involved to shape strategy
- apply imagination and creativity to gaining competitive advantage

Following these principles will provide a solid foundation for strategies that will work; however, it is worth bearing in mind that all business strategy depends on the effectiveness of people in implementing it, and many great plans have been left in shreds by misunderstandings, incompetence and downright cussedness. Recruitment, enablement and motivation of the human resource is the most critical aspect in ensuring strategic and business success.

Implementation, Monitoring and Management

Many international business strategies evolve over years of error, misunderstanding, trial and hope, bringing grey hair to CEOs and multiple stress to corporate executives. The WRAP process circumvents much of this, or rather, absorbs it in the process rather than in the field, but the moment always arrives when the developed strategies need to be implemented.

This is where the real test for the effectiveness of the process lies, as the work done and information developed during the ascent of the WRAP stairway should be sufficiently detailed to avoid the known pitfalls, yet broad enough to allow some leeway for as yet unknown factors to affect the ultimate strategy. To paraphrase this, it can be suggested that only known factors can be evaluated during the course of the process, yet the process is itself designed to identify and make known as many critical factors as possible.

For example, a company in the leather goods industry may have focused its strategic priorities on Eastern Europe. The WRAP process should have identified the key legal, regulatory, market and competitive issues relating to each priority territory as well as the nature and size of the business opportunity. The strategy might suggest that the most effective market access would be gained through acquisition of a local company. But if insufficient research has been put into determining the nature of local companies, this becomes an unknown factor which might, not uncommonly, reveal a tale of small family units interested only in handing their businesses down the inheritance chain. A rapid review of the alternative strategic options would then require to be undertaken.

Once the strategy is effectively implemented, the management of international business becomes an issue of control and information, just like domestic business. The major difference, however, is that many companies delegate these critical management tasks to their local representatives such as distributors or agents, whose agenda does not align with the company's requirements. In practice, a non-exclusive distributor will generally prefer to sell those products in his range that provide him with the highest margins and will focus his sales force accordingly, and thus the company's success in his territory becomes dependent on the distributor's strategy for his own organization. An exclusive distributor or representative, on the other hand, will find it in his or her own best interests to ensure that sales are made to look as grand as possible in the prevailing market conditions, and unless there exists some independent information on the way the market is developing it will be difficult to ascertain whether or not the company's products are being effectively represented.

The WRAP process can help take the organization into the world of international business with as much risk avoidance and priority focus as possible; it makes no sense thereafter to abandon its principles in the longer term as the organization develops its global presence, and that means that success in international business requires well-resourced and focused management, an independent ability to monitor activities, and a continuing commitment to maximizing corporate benefit.

Figure 2.5   Laboratory IT Systems

A small firm, whose sales had so far been entirely confined to its domestic market, sought to find export markets to increase its overseas presence and generate higher revenues for a product that was fully developed. The directors were aware that their system was not easily amenable to language translation and therefore the first criteria selected was that the market required to be English-speaking, at least on screen. The company also feared retaliation from its larger competitors and so the second criteria was that there should be little presence of these companies in the selected export territories. Other criteria included some amenability of business cultures, high-growth potential and prospects for development of related laboratory systems.

Geographic parameters could be said to be almost self-selecting, although there are territories that will adapt to English-language screen definitions in which English is not necessarily the local language.

By these criteria, of course, most of the developed world would not represent appropriate targets as the company's competitors, who, often larger and more dynamic, were present in some force, and thus it was quickly apparent that the list of excluded territories was far longer than the list of potential markets. However, because these laboratory systems were linked to laboratory analyzers, a fruitful source of information on newer and emerging markets were the manufacturers of these products and an interesting pattern began to emerge in which many small countries would accept English-language screens largely because there were no translation packages available for their own language. The downside is that these countries generally showed low growth and limited market potential, although Finland and some others appeared to provide some opportunity.

The answer came as more and more countries were matched against the criteria and turned out to be India, which offered high volume growth in its private health sector, adopted English as its key screen language, and contained sufficient comparability of law and culture to appear as a viable contender. The size of the market in India, within a relatively short time-frame, would be larger than most of the developed countries.

The interesting feature of the example in Figure 2.5 is that the result came from a continual and rational process of matching criteria against key information on a country-by-country basis in a logical and progressive fashion. Although other markets seemed viable, India was prioritized as ultimately the almost ideal example.

3
International Business Cultures

The importance of cultural awareness and sensitivity in international business is a topic that has received a major airing over the past decade, as both managers and academics have made a greater effort to understand the role of cultural issues in developing business and personal relationships and to apply these insights to real-life situations. The literature on the topic is diverse and runs the gamut from in-depth cultural treatises to practical 'how to' books providing guidance on business practices, negotiating styles, and social behavior in specific countries. And the publications have had some positive impact, for it is less usual these days to encounter anyone with any connection to international business who does not have at least a rudimentary grasp of etiquette and basic business practice in markets in which they have an interest.

Cultural awareness, however, entails something more profound than an appreciation of basic courtesy. It also suggests a more mature comprehension of the way individuals living and working within a particular culture think about the world and the things that happen in it, the assumptions they make about the way that world does and should work, and how they are likely to react when presented with particular situations. This also takes in what might be referred to as the cultural infrastructure of a territory, or the tangible manifestations of a culture as exemplified by such things as the local legal and regulatory systems and the language or languages in use in a territory.

There are two assumptions about international business that arise repeatedly, and that often do more to confuse the issue than to pro-vide enlightenment. The first assumption is that newcomers to international business should gain experience in countries with a cultural or business background similar to that of their own country.

Ostensibly, this appears to be a sensible plan: in theory it should be possible to minimize any culture shock while maximizing the development of skills in non-domestic markets, which will then be transferable to new markets. Unfortunately, this takes little account of the harder business reasons for market entry or avoidance and provides minimal scope for applying resource prioritization based on the rational assessment of objectives. If the territory assessed to be most 'similar' actually provides a mediocre market for a product or service, the resultant learning curve may consume a great deal of investment without providing a corresponding return. If the organization is satisfied that the long-term benefits of this approach are likely to outweigh the short-term impact on the profit margin, this may well be a useful way to proceed in developing international markets. The essential point is to understand the ramifications of such decisions.

It is also arguable how similar another cultural environment can ever be. A territory may display retailing practices or a distribution structure closely resembling those in the domestic market, but methods of negotiation or ways of making purchasing decisions may be entirely different. In fact, there exists a counter-argument contending that the most difficult and unfamiliar national market should be attacked first: having exposed the management team to the complexities of a radically different business environment, opening subsequent new markets becomes a comparatively simple task. At US based Applied Materials, CEO Jim Morgan has argued that the managerial and cultural skills developed through breaking into the Japanese market, widely reputed to be the most difficult in the world for almost any product or service, will in fact ease the organization's ability to access other markets in Europe, Asia, or North America.[1]

It is perhaps best to approach this idea with caution. Such an approach requires a management team with substantial experience of cross-cultural business to drive the project carefully and ensure that relationships in the Japanese market are developed and handled appropriately. Applied Materials benefits from a multinational management team with significant international experience, and frankly these abilities are not available in every organization. If the organization's internal capabilities make this a valid approach, then it may be worth considering, but with very great care.

A second assumption about international business centers on the idea that the globalization of trade, product development, and brand management makes local cultures more susceptible to the adoption of foreign products that are not culturally specific or locally produced. For a wide range of products and services this is certainly true, not only of global consumer brands but for critical business products and services such as IT development or manufacturing equipment. In practice, however, successful global branding may mask a high degree of unevenness in customer motivation and expectations.

This chapter is not intended to function as a complete exposition of global cultural complexity, which would require many separate volumes to do the subject justice and is beyond the scope of this chapter. Experience has shown us that many international managers are expected to work across a variety of cultures and territories over time, even though they may have a long-term focus on a few significant territories. Our intention is to equip the reader with ways of recognizing and thinking about cultural issues and their effect on the customer base and the business process, and by extension on the development and implementation of successful international strategy.

This is a good time to recall an observation made in Chapter One. You may not like everything you see around you, it may not make rational sense to you in the first instance, or it may inspire you with frustration. This is natural, but that is not the point. The things that happen in any part of the world happen for a reason, and it is up to the responsible manager to understand the prevailing logic and work within it, or more precisely, to endeavor to make it work for the organization rather than against it.

Cultural priorities

Despite the variety of cultural and social contexts encountered in global markets, there are common denominators across cultures: for example, all human cultures have been observed to engage in trade and various forms of reciprocal exchange, and possess notions of rights and obligations.[2] Ethnographic observations aside, it is useful to assume that individuals conduct business for a reason. In the modern world this is most likely to be with the aim of making money, although the profit imperative may also be accompanied by a desire to gain influence or prestige through business dealings.

The influence of culture on strategy and management takes two different forms. Culture obviously has a profound influence on the potential customer base, particularly the way customers make decisions about purchasing goods and services. In addition it is, or should be, a determiner of effective management style and practice when working closely with partners or employees with a background in a foreign culture. This is especially true when setting up a direct operation or joint venture in a foreign market, or making an acquisition that will ultimately be managed by or responsible to foreign nationals.

Is it necessary to take culture into consideration when formulating international corporate strategy? There exists an argument that it is not at all necessary. According to this approach, strategy is a summation of corporate objectives and how they will be delivered, and these objectives exist independently of cultural variations and are not affected by them. Strategy implementation is likely in practice to require some response to cultural variables, but this does not affect the validity of the strategy itself.

When utilizing the WRAP process, however, culture becomes a critical aspect of strategy development through its impact on corporate objectives themselves. The process of market assessment, covered in Chapter 6, in part helps to identify key cultural issues that may affect the operation of the market itself, and influence the organization's ability to respond successfully to the demands of the market. This in turn may influence the adjustment of corporate objectives to take account of realities on the ground. It is in this sense that culture has a direct impact on strategy: it is important to take culture related issues into account in order to arrive at an adequate assessment of potential performance and risk and to gain an understanding of what can realistically be achieved in global markets in order to set realistic and achievable strategic objectives. Further down the line, the implementation of international strategy is also partly dependent on an appreciation of, as well as an ability to respond to and utilize, cultural differences across and within national territories.

In our experience, the growth in awareness of business cultures has resulted in an interesting phenomenon. Managers arrive in another country with business cards printed in two languages, prepared to bow, remove their shoes, eat unusual foods, and generally do their utmost to accommodate themselves appropriately to the local culture. However, in many cases they subsequently fail to appreciate that the structure and operation of the market may be entirely different from that they are used to at home, and consequently requires a different set of responses in order to secure satisfactory organizational performance. There appears in some instances to be a lack of clear awareness of the way culture interacts with the mechanisms of the market to produce a unique environment that has strategic as well as tactical significance.

This is often borne out by the experiences of businesses operating on the ground. For example, in some Arab territories the provision of services and operation of business within the country is influenced or controlled by a small number of families. In some cases, the country as a whole operates as a type of 'family business' in which a network of brothers, uncles and cousins effectively manage access to a wide range of market opportunities, whether in the private or public sector. In such a situation it is imperative to get along with, or at the very least not alienate, key figures in the these families in order to establish or maintain a presence in the territory. Similarly, Korean industry is dominated by the chaebol, the highly diversified multinational firms that are represented in almost every segment of the Korean market and which effectively operate as a gateway to diverse market segments.

A variety of frameworks have been developed to aid the international manager, or other interested party, to achieve a more constructive comprehension of foreign cultures. These include the 'cultural metaphors' of Gannon[3], which are intended to locate a culture within a matrix or continuum of characteristics. This is in turn designed to assist the observer in identifying cultural priorities and arriving at a

Figure 3.1   The End

Contracting public services to foreign companies is not unheard of in many territories, and the Middle East is no exception. The government (actually the ruling family) of a Middle East territory contracted with a British company to build and operate a large general hospital in the capital city, employing mainly expatriate doctors and nurses and provided health services to a range of local patients. The firm operating the contract had made a strategic decision to compete in Middle Eastern healthcare markets, identifying a growing market for managed healthcare services in this region.

The hospital was well equipped and staffed by highly trained medical personnel, but operated for several years at extremely high cost to the government. This issue was raised many times but still the costs rose until the point was reached where it was cheaper to send the local patients to private hospitals and clinics in Europe and the United States. As patient numbers at the hospital began to drop the management raised prices yet again to allow for underutilization of its equipment and resources, and the inevitable happened. The contract was canceled and the firm was given three months' notice to move out. The company was preparing to sue the Middle Eastern government for breach of contract until it was gently reminded that not only was its pricing well beyond the contract agreement, but also that the ultimate court of appeal in this country was the head of the ruling family, who owned the hospital and canceled the contract.

Of course other governments in the region, suffering from similar cost difficulties with the company, noted the decision and also canceled their contracts. The company withdrew completely from the area but found that it could not compete elsewhere, as its management was inefficient and thus required high pricing to cover their shortcomings. It's a sad end for a failed strategy, but the company simply had no idea of the business risks it was running by taking selfish advantage of the natural politeness and courtesy of its hosts and their unwillingness to create bad feeling.

basic cultural orientation in an unfamiliar cultural landscape. Similarly, the 'dilemma reconciliation' proposed by Trompenaars offers a method of overcoming the negative feedback generated by culture clash through identifying points of conflict and endeavoring to utilize these in a more positive manner.

Whether the relevant representative of an unfamiliar culture is a colleague, a partner or a customer, it is likely that their cultural priorities will differ significantly from those that exist in the organization's domestic market. The way these priorities are worked out in practice within the culture may not be immediately obvious; it is also the case the priorities can vary within a culture, with different considerations taking precedence as new situations arise, as exemplified in Figure 3.2. The increasingly global nature of trade and business has prompted some discussion about issues of cultural relativity, or how far an individual can or should adapt their behavior and organizational operations to the social and moral values of the society in which they happen to be doing business. The standard advice is for managers to remain 'centered', although centered on exactly what is not always clear.

In one sense, of course, culture *is* relative. Acceptable, or more to the point constructive and profitable, forms of behavior and management style are in fact dependent to some degree on local practice, which

Figure 3.2 Walk This Way

In Muslim communities that adhere to a more strict interpretation of traditional Islamic social and moral codes, men are observed to take precedence over women in most public and private interactions. Women in traditional dress cover their heads, and possibly their faces and much of the rest of their bodies, and may also be expected to walk behind a male relative in public. To all intents and purposes, the man appears to be incontrovertibly in charge.

Visibly at least, this was the relationship that existed between mother and son at a family owned food processing company in Egypt. Mother followed son into the factory in the morning, followed him home in the evening, cooked the meal, attended to his requirements, and made sure that he was a relaxed and contented member of the society. However, during the hours of business mother took control: she had more experience than her son and was a sharper negotiator, and it was common for men in the firm, family members or not, to defer to her superior awareness of the business environment when making decisions about the direction of the company.

This is a pattern not anomalous in traditional Muslim societies. Women are expected to defer to men in many situations and do not have the ostensible freedom of activity taken for granted by women in Western societies, but it is a mistake to discount their influence altogether. In business or professional situations women may carry as much, if not more, status as the men behind whom they walk.

determines what the locals expect of one another, and by extension are likely to expect of foreign colleagues. This has a concomitant impact on the expectations and reactions of the management back at headquarters, wherever that may be, which may make it seem like a full time job simply mediating between cultural mores. Nevertheless, accepting the existence of conceptual constraints on both sides is fundamental to identifying ways to move beyond these limitations.

Figure 3.3   Three Imperatives of Cultural Awareness

1. *Be aware of the potential for cultural difference.* Expect it to materialize. Look out for it actively. Seek advice and listen to it.
2. *Respect these differences.* Reluctance to engage with different cultures and lifestyles is ultimately counterproductive.
3. *Assess their implications.* Cultural differences can provide areas of . opportunity as well as constraint. Find a way to ground organizational aspirations and goals and those of colleagues in country in a common framework that respects the local business and cultural environment while enabling the organization to rationally address its objectives.

Key cultural characteristics of the marketplace

It is useful to bear in mind that a spectrum of opinion exists within countries on a whole range of topics, whether or not this is openly expressed on editorial pages or current affairs programs. The likelihood is that not everybody agrees with absolutely everything that takes place in their own country, and whether or not they are free to say so they are still constrained to work within these systems themselves.

Language and communication

This is generally the first issue that springs to mind when companies begin to think about getting involved in non-domestic markets. It also seems to be the first stumbling block when it comes to organizing a practical and workable approach to the market, because the question of who needs or is able to speak which language seems to create a great deal of unnecessary confusion in the minds of some managers.

It is true to say that the language of international business is English. It is currently the most widely spoken second language in the world, and everyone with serious ambitions to participate directly in the global economy will have at least a basic knowledge of English. However, recall our client from Chapter One, whose English language sales force was on a mission to sell capital equipment to German engineers. In fact many German engineers speak excellent English, but when it's a question of discussing technical requirements or parting with a six figure sum for a complex piece of machinery, they quite naturally prefer to do so in the comfort and security of their native language. This is true across the whole range of industries and products, from the highly technical down to the simplest goods.

However, the most important aspect of the language issue is also the one that is most frequently overlooked. In global markets, language is about communication, and communication is part of the wider issue of demonstrating credibility within the marketplace. Fluency itself is not enough to crack the market.

It is useful to have practical experience of conducting business in the territory, and to have contacts in-country who are familiar with the industry or market and know how it operates locally, without having to learn everything from scratch. It is also helpful to consider the specific attributes or connections that contribute most to gaining credibility in a given market, such as specific educational qualifications or membership of professional bodies, which are recognizable in the territory and enhance professional status. In short, language skills are only one aspect of the wider problem of creating a presence that is understood and respected in a potential market.

Linguistic expertise is a skill that can be bought and sold like any other, and when it is bought in it should preferably be allied to market experience and contacts to provide a more comprehensive method of managing communication and credibility. It's not just about speaking: it is about presenting the company and its offering in such a way that it commands attention.

Regionalization

The prioritization of a national market does not necessarily indicate that the entire territory is a uniform market. Many territories display at least some degree of regional disparity that may have a direct impact on decisions relating to sales and marketing or the siting of a manufacturing facility or the organization of a joint venture or acquisition. Understanding the dynamics of regional organization can make geographically large markets, such as the United States or China, or even Spain or Germany, much more manageable in the first instance, and provide an entry point for testing the market and assessing the potential of a carefully chosen portion of the territory before committing more substantial resources to it.

There are various types of regionalization that exist to some degree in many territories worldwide. Ethnic or cultural regionalization recognizes a cleavage between certain groups of people living within one nation, which may be more or less significant depending on their respective historical backgrounds. This may overlap with additional linguistic or religious divisions. On a less personal level, market or industry regionalization focuses on the geographic niche market for a product or service. A target customer base may be concentrated in one or more specific areas that display such characteristics as higher median incomes, or that host a cluster of companies focused on a particular industry sector. Depending on the size of the country, it may be most effective to concentrate the initial market entry program in or near these regions before extending organizational presence to the rest of the territory.

It is also possible for the different types of regionalization to overlap. For example, Spain has three major cultural regions with corresponding industry profiles: the Basque Country, which is the traditional home of heavy industries such as steel and machine tool production, Catalonia, which has a contemporary concentration of lighter, high-tech industry, and Castilian Spain with a widely dispersed base of modern industry including aerospace and automotive manufacturing. Companies in any or all of these regions may be purchasing the same things, but in many cases it is unrealistic to expect one organization to sell equally effectively to all of them. The Basque may have few or no market contacts in Catalonia, and the individual working out of Madrid may have difficulty establishing credibility in Barcelona. In practice, a Spanish distributor will address this issue by contracting with sub-distributors throughout the country in order to ensure that any regional differences are handled appropriately.

Religion and belief

Far from being a system of abstract beliefs with little application in everyday life, religion in its broad sense can have a pervasive influence on everything from lifestyle to political structures. Many countries and tribal areas follow religious-based practices with a fervor uncommon among the more sceptical developed economies, ranging from fundamentalist Christian catholic and evangelical beliefs to Judaism, Hindu, and pagan beliefs. These can also be bound together with forms of cultural or state nationalism which offer some protection for these beliefs in a secular or irreligious world.

At present this appears to be most widely evident in territories with a predominantly Muslim population, where both business practices and lifestyle choices may be deeply conditioned by religious considerations.

For example, the working week in a Muslim country runs from Saturday to Thursday to allow for the Friday religious holiday. In those countries with a legal system based on Shari'a law, a very rigorous observation of religious principles is not uncommon. In Saudi Arabia customs authorities strictly enforce regulations regarding the import of goods considered to be contrary to the tenets of Islam, such as alcohol, pork products, pornography, and non-Islamic religious material. However, these regulations have also been broadly interpreted to include less obviously unacceptable items such as Christmas decorations and fashion magazines.

Identifying and managing issues arising from religious affiliation may be neither easy nor obvious, but the failure to do so may have a substantive impact on the acceptability of the organization or product in the designated market. These problems may come to the fore in consumer markets, where personal allegiances and preferences may take greater precedence over issues of utility and cost, but they cannot be entirely ruled out in business-to-business markets in regions where religious tensions habitually run high.

Figure 3.4 The Colors of Charity

A UK-wide charity with its headquarters in London had become aware, quite correctly, that its fund-raising activities in Scotland needed to be treated as distinct from those in the rest of the UK. For example, Scottish donors to charities often prefer to support organizations that specify that monies raised will be spent within Scotland itself, and charitable bequests within wills may make the legacy conditional on where the money is to be used.

The charity accordingly planned a fund-raising campaign focused around its activities in Scotland. A combined letter and brochure with an orange color scheme were designed in London with the aim of attracting contributions across the entire spectrum of the community, and were subsequently sent to the local office in Scotland for final approval before a mass mailing was carried out. This was just as well, for the designers had failed to observe the proviso that had repeatedly been handed back by their Scottish colleagues: by all means use color, but not orange or green. Sectarian tensions in parts of Scotland between Protestants and Catholics makes the use of these colors, more commonly association with religious conflict in Northern Ireland, problematic and in this case risked raising entirely unnecessary questions about whether the charity was actively 'taking sides' in an area where local tensions can be exacerbated by religious affiliation.

Geography, infrastructure and climate

The sheer size of some countries has clear implications for logistics arrangements, but these can be complicated by additional difficulties. In some large developing countries regional distributors or agents may be difficult to find, which may in turn necessitate the delivery of products direct to customers over long distances. This can be made more problematic by infrastructure issues such as poor quality roads, resulting in slower transport and potential product damage.

Depending on the nature of the product or service and the territory in which it is being sold, it may also be useful to ascertain the quality of other aspects of the physical infrastructure, such as reliable supplies of power and water, or communication networks of an appropriate standard. This may become critical in cases in which products require storage in an air-conditioned environment, or suffer operational damage from electricity surges or cuts that may be commonplace in the region.

Climatic conditions in some territories, particularly those prone to high heat and humidity, may be a cause of unexpected product deterioration that applies to a far wider range of products than food and drink. It is important in such instances to ensure that any stock held in-country is stored under appropriate conditions and that associated transportation and distribution arrangements take account of these problems. It may also be necessary to examine any customer service and support on offer to ensure that it is responsive to situations that arise in this context.

Figure 3.5 Climate Change

A range of tropical countries in Africa and Southeast Asia provided target markets for a European healthcare company offering a range of disposable bedpans made out of specially treated paper. These had been successfully supplied to hospitals in developed countries, and the company believed that the bedpans would prove an easy and inexpensive means of improving hygiene in territories with a lower per capita expenditure on healthcare.

Unfortunately, these good intentions were defeated by the tropical climate, in which high humidity is a regular fact of life. The humidity accelerated the degradation of the paper bedpans even as they sat in storage. Once in use, the additional moisture coming into contact with the bedpans caused them to suffer what might best be described as catastrophic failure. This spelled the end of the disposable bedpan in the tropics.

A similar humidity induced problem occurred in Thailand, where industrial machinery made of metal was shipped in from the European Union and stored in a warehouse lacking any form of climate control. The machinery rapidly began to rust in the humid atmosphere. Although this did not result in any immediate technical failure, the machinery appeared at least superficially to have deteriorated by the time it reached the customer, creating a poor impression and encouraging customers to lend their attention to competitors with a sharper image.

Legal and regulatory issues

Recognition of the diversity of legal and regulatory frameworks is a critical aspect of operating in non-domestic markets. Most sovereign states have a defined legal code in operation within their boundaries, but this may be overlaid or supplemented by separate state, provincial or regional codes or systems. In addition, supranational organizations such as the European Union pass legislation applicable in many cases to all member countries, as do international bodies such as the World Trade Organization. Regulatory codes may apply to situations specific to particular industry sectors or to broader issues such as environmental protection or health and safety at work, and may also be promulgated at various levels.

- *Import controls.* Import controls encompass tariffs, customs duties, import licenses, and other measures intended to regulate or prohibit entry of goods. Import prohibitions may also be put in place out of consideration for the maintenance of health, safety, or environmental standards in the importing country, or as a means of endeavoring to force other territories to adopt these standards. Import controls include protectionist industry barriers that restrict foreign competition with domestic industries on other grounds. The US defense industry in a primary example of this practice: many defense systems are produced according to a 'no foreign content' rule that prohibits the use of imported components in their manufacture. This rule does not, however, bar foreign companies from establishing a base in the US and servicing such contracts with American staff and locally manufactured products.
- *Export controls.* Restrictions or prohibitions may be placed on the export of certain categories of goods and services from a territory. This is most often an issue where the national security or foreign policy aims of the territorial government are perceived to be affected by supplies to another country, or where such supplies are considered to have a potentially negative impact on internationally accepted human rights or non-proliferation agreements. For example, the US government places export controls on new, or what it considers to be secret, technology that bans its transfer to any other country, thus maintaining the nation's perceived edge in national defense.
- *Standards.* Standards relating to product quality and safety are often established to assure consumers and workers of minimum quality standards covering relevant products sold in the region. For example, in the European Union the CE mark covers a wide range of products and is intended to certify conformity with health, safety, and environmental regulations. Although standards often function

as legal requirements for market entry, non-mandatory standards or codes of practice may be promulgated by industry or professional associations as voluntary evidence of good practice. Standards of this type may offer valuable marketing support on a local basis.

- *Packaging and labeling.* Packaging and labeling requirements may encompass environmental, safety, and information issues. The question of packaging waste and its disposal or recycling has also become more prominent in recent years.
- *Intellectual property.* Intellectual property rights, or IPR's, cover acknowledgment of and reimbursement for patented or copyrighted inventions, designs, or other works. These rights are supported by the World Trade Organization and should be enforced by member countries, but in practice this is dependent in part on the reliability of the domestic legal system. In countries with less robust legal systems, violation of IPRs may be difficult to prosecute successfully. Such violations may pose serious competitive or financial problems for the organization on a territorial or even global basis.
- *Corporate ownership.* Foreign ownership of local business entities may be restricted or limited in some way, either broadly or in specific sectors.
- *Tax and accounting.* It is important to take professional advice to ensure compliance with local accounting procedures and tax codes as they apply to the organization's local activities. This includes any liability for value added tax, sales tax, stamp duty or similar assessments.

The legal and regulatory framework in a territory is important not only because of the desirability of avoiding prosecution in a criminal or civil court. It also has a critical effect on the level of risk inherent in market entry, determining how effectively an organization is able to carry out its business and protect its interests through reliance on the legal system, without resorting to costly and probably dangerous sub-legal expedients.

For example, there may exist the problem of an insufficient or incomplete legal structure, as evidenced by many countries moving from a command to a market economy. The existing legal structure in such territories is often not well adapted to contract law, or to the adjudication of other business-related disputes. Consequently, agreements concluded in the country may be difficult to enforce, and the obscurity or complete lack of legal precedents is likely to make any resulting lawsuit hard to win even with sound local legal representation. This obviously increases the risk of market entry to at least some degree, but this may be acceptable to the organization depending on the identified potential of the market to deliver on corporate objectives.

Allied to the question of legal position is that of government structure and continuity, determining which policies are likely to be supported and carried out. This often has a bearing on the business climate, given that governments promulgate laws and direct their enforcement, or mastermind regulations designed to encourage or constrain businesses operating within their political remit. This may impact either directly or more informally on the ability to do business in a territory.

Political continuity also has a profound impact on economic and legal stability, but this may in practice manifest itself in less obvious ways. Many American managers are somewhat nervous of the Italian market, often on the assumption that perceived political instability in the country increases market risk. It is true that Italian governments since 1945 have lasted for around a year each, which bears little resemblance to the reliable four-year terms of US administrations. Although the governments may come and go, however, the civil servants live on to administer, regulate, enforce, and organize, providing a continuity that is not always evident on the political scene.

Before supplying goods or services to a territory it is advisable to seek specific advice on applicable legal and regulatory issues. It is often possible to obtain guidance not only from local legal professionals, but from the commercial sections of embassies and consulates in the country. Relevant trade associations representing the nation's domestic suppliers or importers are often a useful source of information on issues specific to industry sectors or particular products.

Business ethics

The advice provided to international managers on the topic of business ethics is generally quite succinct. It is observed that there is 'plenty of opportunity for ethical decision-making' in global markets, and that responsible managers should be prepared to 'act as their own policeman'. In essence, these are different ways of expressing the need for judgment to be applied to situations that are by their nature often unclear.

In the first instance it is important to understand the organization's legal position, both within a specific territory and externally. Some countries, such as the US, promulgate laws that specifically regulate corporate behavior, and by extension the behavior of individual managers, in foreign territories with the aim of reducing corruption. Individual countries may also have laws on the books that specifically address the behavior of foreign companies or nationals doing business in the territory, or it may be the case that general national laws are applied to 'make an example' of foreign business people falling foul of national anti-corruption legislation. In any case, it is the responsibility of the individual and their employer to know, understand and work within the legal framework in the territory in which they operate.

Beyond this, it is useful to recognize a continuum of practices that are likely to be encountered in various parts of the world, understanding that what is acceptable in one territory may be anathema in another. To take one example, the principle of competitive business practice, which is generally assumed to be fundamental to capitalist (or at least market-oriented) economies, may not take an identical form in every territory, or it may be subverted by alternate cultural priorities. Globally, not all business transactions operate on a strictly competitive basis in which the lowest bid or the largest discount wins the tender, or where the contract is awarded to the product or service offering that demonstrably best meets the buyer's perceived requirements.

In some territories, the concept of 'fairness' takes priority over strict competition. Contracts from government departments or large state-owned enterprises may be awarded to suppliers or agents on a rolling basis, with each one taking it in turn to supply required products or services. This is often viewed as a method of ensuring that everyone in the industry is able to make a reasonable living by having a regular, reliable opportunity to supply at least some products.

Allied to the concept of fairness is the desire to provide family support through a business. An enterprise may be expected to provide a living for an extended family, for example by means of a product distributorship that is operated through a network of family members, rather than through a specially selected range of sub-distributors strategically located throughout the country. Rather than being seen simply as crude nepotism, this can be regarded as a responsible approach to the demands of both business and family in a location where the population outstrips the opportunities for earning even a small income.

Similarly, the problem of bribery or 'backhanders' is usually associated in Western minds with developing economies, although in practice it can arise anywhere, prompted by a range of business or personal interactions. Bribery is often viewed by Western businesspeople as an irresponsible, not to mention illegal, effort to extort money for services that should be provided free as a matter of course, or at a lower cost. It may take diverse forms, from bribing government officials in order to obtain contracts all the way down to low-level anomalies such as paying airport staff to release suitcases from the baggage claim. Many governments have made and continue to make active efforts to stamp out corrupt practices. However, bribery can have another dimension to those who are involved in it. In a territory such as India where a very large proportion of the population live in extreme poverty without a clear or reliable means of making a living, such payments may mean that an individual and their family are able to survive more successfully than they would by relying entirely on straightforward income.

There is also the concept of favors, in which a friend or colleague takes the opportunity to repay a previous friendly gesture. Terminologically this falls under the general saying 'you scratch my back and I'll scratch yours', which stems from the practice among many animals of helping remove the mites and fleas from each other's inaccessible places. In human terms this covers many circumstances in which some of the most prominent opportunities might include seeking some commercial return for political party or election donations or taking up supplier invitations to visit them (at their expense) at some exotic location.

The preceding observations are not intended to excuse or condone these or any other practices, but to acknowledge their existence and illuminate issues, such as poverty or genuine differences in ethical perceptions or social organization, that are often inseparable from the ethical dilemmas encountered by international managers.

Security and threat assessment

The question of personal and business security in the global marketplace has taken on a particular resonance in the post 9/11 climate of comparative uncertainty and instability on political, military, and economic fronts. It is no longer simply a matter of staying away from the world's documented hotspots, since it now appears to be possible for terrorist attacks to overtake the business or leisure traveler even in locations previously believed to be more or less free from such risks. In practice such attacks are rare and the chances of being caught up in one are extremely small. Nevertheless, when potential threats may be poorly identified and sound information about them is scarce, it is difficult to realistically assess the risk that the organization runs through maintaining presence in a particular territory.

Physical security issues relate to the safety of individuals or property in foreign territories. This takes in first of all basic street crime, extending in some territories to more uncommon threats. Foreign businesspeople and their commercial interests are perhaps most likely to be caught up indirectly in civil unrest or terrorist incidents, and even where there is no direct harm done to the business such situations may depress the market and make it difficult to carry out business in the normal fashion. It is also possible for foreigners and their interests to be targeted directly, either as a protest against an organization itself and its activities in the territory, or as a blow against perceived foreign influence from a specific country or countries. Figure 3.6 lists a range of potential physical threats in order of escalating severity.

Figure 3.6 Physical Threats

Nature of risk	Implications
Street crime	Exists to some degree in both cities and rural areas worldwide, with actual risk depending on local circumstances.
Health-related issues	Includes limited-term but severe epidemics such as SARS, and endemic health risks such as malaria and parasitic diseases. Food poisoning is relatively common in some areas.
Political instability	Weak central government may be challenged by a defined faction or by a more loosely organized group of insurgents whose aim may be the violent overthrow of the government.
Terrorist targeting	Terrorist activity may be tied to a localized dispute, or a threat may be posed by 'international' terrorists whose aims may encompass disruption of a wide range of targets across many countries.
Kidnapping	Expatriate workers or local colleagues may be kidnapped either as a means of extorting ransom, or in order to undermine the organization's local operations.

Apart from physical violence, threat assessment also addresses the wider financial and economic risks of international business that can have an unexpected impact on organizations operating outside their home territory. Economic risk and threat assessment recognizes that the organization may be adversely affected by financial and economic issues beyond its control, and that the nature and severity of these problems influences decisions about market entry and exit.

Figure 3.7 Examples of Economic Risk

Nature of risk	Implications
Organized crime	Businesses may attract demands from local criminals for 'protection' money; alternately, organized criminals may endeavor to restrict market access entirely
Currency fluctuations	Profit can quickly disappear or costs rise substantially
Payment terms	Failure by the customer to adhere to the agreed terms is common and recourse to law is not always the best solution; also, payment cycles can be very long or irregular
Customer failure or departure	Should be covered by credit insurance

Threat assessment is an essential aspect of understanding and managing market risk. A rational assessment of these issues allows the organization to draw realistic conclusions about the levels of risk inherent in physical and economic threats, and to take steps wherever possible to ameliorate such risk or alternately, if this is not feasible, to exit the market. A useful point of first contact in assessing these risks is the domestic embassy or consulate in the foreign territory, which should have up-to-date information on existing physical or economic risks in the country.

Finally, there is also a risk in overplaying security issues and allowing them to unduly restrict international activity. If it is just conceivable that an individual could be a victim of a terrorist attack while on business in a foreign country, it is much more likely that they would be hit by a car while crossing the street. As always, the best approach is to avoid panic.

Notes

1 Fons Trompenaars, *Did The Pedestrian Die?* p. 43
2 Donald E. Brown's List of Human Universals, Appendix, *The Blank Slate*, Steven Pinker, London: Penguin, 2002.
3 Martin J. Gannon, *Understanding Global Cultures*, Sage Publications, 2001.

4
Understanding International Customers

The concept of market-led strategy naturally presupposes a requirement for some degree of knowledge of the markets targeted for development. Every market is made up of variable components and can be influenced by a swathe of external factors. Sitting at the core of all this dynamism is that elusive being, the customer, the one who is fundamental to the existence of the market in the first place. The use of the term 'elusive' is entirely deliberate in this context. In fact, there are few questions so challenging and difficult to resolve as these: What is my real customer base? And what makes them *my* customers, rather than someone else's?

When there is something to sell, ideally there exists someone on the other end to buy whatever it is on offer, but the path from one to the other may vary quite considerably depending on how it is actually mapped out. The idea of customer awareness takes on a particular importance in international markets. Apart from governments and large public bodies, and globally concentrated industries such as energy, there are few conveniently managed monolithic international sectors in which similar types of people follow a standardized logic to arrive at easily comprehensible decisions. Customer behavior and expectations are highly frangible concepts that may vary significantly not only between territories, but also within them, and for reasons that may not be immediately obvious.

Despite all the hype about 'globalization', with its populist implications of market and product standardization on a Western model, there is no future in waiting hopefully for the homogenization of a global customer base. It may well be that, in some cases, customers around the world are buying similar products or services. However, the train of choices and requirements that leads to that ultimate purchasing decision may differ radically from one territory to the next, and the range of uses and benefits that the customer expects from their purchase may be equally diverse. The implication is clear: it is important to know *what* the customer is buying, but it is equally important to understand *why* and *how* they choose to buy it. Or indeed, why they don't bother to buy it at all.

In practice, the considerations that drive foreign customers to behave in the way that they do may not differ markedly from those that obtain in the domestic market. What is important is to establish *whether* and *how* customer motivations differ. This dictates the way in which an organization can best approach the market: what types of products stand the best chance of success, which routes to market will prove most productive, and how profitable the territorial venture will ultimately prove to be.

Understanding customer motivation and the way it changes is critical to unlocking the potential of non-domestic markets and developing them over the longer term. It allows the seller to tap into the dynamics of the market and understand not only how they can respond to market demand, but ultimately how they can endeavor to drive and shape the market over time. Of course, customer motivation is likely to have at least something to do with the cultural context in which it takes place. In terms of the sale of food products or consumer electronics, the cultural background of the potential customer base may have a huge influence on product acceptability. By contrast, if it is a question of supplying aerospace components or equipment for electronics manufacturing, it is likely that considerations not directly related to national culture will assume at least equal prominence in the mind of the buyer.

Customer motivation and cultural context, while being related concepts that do overlap to some extent, are not identical and merit a separate analysis. The cultural context in which business takes place in any market is likely to be more continuous and change more slowly and incrementally over time. Customer motivation is naturally conditioned by the cultural context within the territory, but it may also be open to the influence of technical, financial, or competitive issues that are not direct products of a given national culture.

Together, these two aspects of the market form a foundation for the successful development of any strategies in foreign markets. It also does no harm to remember that someone, somewhere, is thinking of almost every organization or individual as *their* foreign customer.

Identifying the real customer base

The structure of the supply chain in a foreign territory is often not so different from that in the domestic market. It is not uncommon for suppliers to make use of distributors or agents in their home territory as a means of benefiting from the distributor's contacts and expertise, or of avoiding investment in a direct sales force, while still maintaining some level of contact with and awareness of their end-user base. This situation can become much more difficult in foreign markets, where direct or indirect contact between the supplier on the one hand, and end-users and their environment on the other, may be sporadic or liable to misunderstanding.

Identifying the real customer base can be especially useful in foreign markets as a means of understanding the behavior and motivations of the various entities that come into contact with a product as it passes through the supply chain. In many cases, it is helpful to make a basic distinction between direct customers and the ultimate end-users of the product or service to be supplied, and to be aware of the ways in which each of them influences the ability of the organization to supply the product successfully in a specific market.

Who is the direct customer? Self-evidently, this is the organization or individual buying products directly. In some cases, as where a direct sales operation is in place, this may in fact be the final end-user, but it is quite likely, particularly in non-domestic markets, that the direct customer is a distributor, agent, or wholesaler who will take responsibility for sales or product placement in the territory. From this point, products work their way through the supply chain until they arrive in the hands of the end-user, who is the individual or organization using or converting the product.

This final customer is the end-user, the one whose existence is ultimately essential in carving out a space in the market. These end-users make the ultimate decisions about which products or services to purchase or reject, how much they want to pay for them, and what level of after-sales service they will expect as an integral part of their purchasing decision. The market is ultimately dependent on them. This seems too obvious to merit discussion until we reflect on the very great deal of confusion often overlaying this issue in practice, particularly in business-to-business markets in which customers themselves may be part of a larger supply chain and need to sell products to their own demanding customers. Direct customers and end-users may have entirely different aims as members of the supply chain, and it is the responsibility of the supplier to understand and work with the dynamics of this relationship.

Differentiation between direct customers and end-users can be a particularly useful tool in situations where distributors buy and hold stock: although products are purchased from the organization, are incorporated into the sales figures, and appear to be moving through the supply chain, they may not be reaching the end-user in anything like the manner or quantity they could be.

It is fundamental to understand that both type of customer exist within their own markets. They may have customers of their own that make certain demands on them, or they may operate within an industry sector in which technical and competitive issues generate separate pressures. This suggests that the direct customer and the end-user may operate in markets that are related but not identical, and will need to be treated as distinct. By doing so, it is possible to identify the locus of decision-making and pursue opportunities to reach the final customer through the appropriate channels.

Drivers in customer market sectors

These issues become clearer as the drivers in customer markets are examined more fully. End-users buy products or services, or decline to buy them, for one or more reasons, and these reasons are intimately tied up with their requirements and needs as customers. The features that are most important to determine are those that drive the final customer to provide a sales opportunity and those that indicate a negative response. Why would they want to buy and use a specific product or service? What would cause them to reject it?

The considerations that influence the purchasing behavior of end-users in any territory, foreign or otherwise, are *customer drivers*. These drivers may be very similar to those at work in the domestic market. However, it is important to be clear about how similar or otherwise these drivers really are, so that their implications can be taken into account and the organization can position itself to address actual market requirements. This helps the organization to avoid one of the common pitfalls of international business: concerning itself only with what it wants to sell, rather than with what the customer would prefer to buy.

This book has been organized so as to separate the cultural characteristics of the marketplace from the discussion of the customer base and its drivers. This is deliberate: by drawing an initial distinction between these two aspects of the market, it is possible to gain a better understanding of how far they overlap, and to what degree culture-specific issues drive customer behavior.

Selected examples of customer drivers are listed in Figure 4.1, including comments indicating how these drivers might operate to affect customer behavior. Customer drivers can encompass almost any aspect of the customer's relationship with the company, its products or services, their method of delivery, or they can arise from issues current in the social, political, or economic environment that may not be directly related to the market at all.

It is also important to recognize that customer drivers are unlikely to be identical across global markets, or to produce uniform outcomes in all territories. An innovative design may attract new customers in one territory, and in another it may be perceived as too complex or alien to customer requirements. Global brand awareness may be a strong selling point, or it may spur customers to seek out less well known local brands as a way of supporting the local economy.

Figure 4.1   Examples of Customer Drivers

Customer drivers	Market considerations
Legal and regulatory requirements	May be unevenly enforced in different territories
Product quality and design	May command premium/lower prices
Brand awareness	May be possible to leverage brand awareness already built up in other territories/may detract from product marketability
Level of technology	Market preference may be for lower-tech or high-tech products
Service and support	Local customer service may be necessary
Competition	Existing competitors may define the market
Pricing	Higher pricing may enhance product status/lower pricing may enhance mass appeal
Profitability	Business customers consider their own bottom line when evaluating products
Cultural preferences	Appeal of product features may vary considerably across territories

Figure 4.2 Driving the Customer

Having earlier examined the role played by cultural and allied considerations in international market development, it is instructive to look at a situation in which a customer driver of this type played an important but diffused role in affecting market demand.

As a component part of a strategy development program, it was necessary to identify the principal customer drivers influencing the use and purchase of British-made machine tools in Italy. This had long been perceived in the industry as a difficult market for UK suppliers. The size and structure of the market were widely appreciated and appeared to offer significant opportunities, but on the whole British manufacturers had found the territory to be a very challenging environment.

Discussions with end-users, distributors, manufacturers, and other market participants turned up a variety of interesting, and not wholly unexpected, factors that affected both the suitability and desirability of machinery supplied from the UK. These included, amongst others, a preference for a comparatively high degree of machine customization, supported by a strong local service presence. In addition, the research turned up another, rather more unusual, circumstance driving the behavior of Italian customers.

In the early 1990s Honda operated a design partnership with Rover in the UK that encompassed the design and production of cars of almost identical specifications, but sporting two different badges. The cars were marketed in the hope that the reputation of, and association with, Japanese engineering and service could lift Rover into contention as a major player in European automotive markets.

Unfortunately, despite offering a virtually identical vehicle, the Honda model outsold Rover 3 to 1 in Italy. How did this arise? In fact, Italian consumers had not yet forgotten the saga of the UK-built Jaguar in the 1980s. This stylish, high-performance car made its biggest impact on Italian drivers through its unreliability. It broke down. It was seen at the side of the autostrada with the hood up, which was far from stylish. It made such an impression that several years later, Italians failed to be swayed by the promotional lure of British branding and Japanese engineering and simply bought the Japanese car.

The denouement of all this was that when they were asked a decade or so later about their perceptions of British quality, Italian engineers remembered the saga of The Cars. Not that they confused cars with machine tools, but their ideas about the reliability of UK-made equipment had to some degree been shaped by their recollections of these problems and the knock-on effects they had produced in the market.

Of course, the issue of automotive reliability described in Figure 4.2 was not entirely responsible for the difficulties experienced by many British companies in the Italian market. But it became important for companies active in the country to work harder to overcome these perceptions as an aspect of their wider marketing program.

Given the fact that such customer drivers may be highly diverse and spring from sources with no apparent connection to the target market, it may appear to be unduly difficult to obtain a comprehensive understanding of these influences. The best way to get to grips with them is, simply, to ask. Ask questions of individuals who are in a position to have a particular knowledge of the market under review, and be sure they are open-ended questions that allow the maximum freedom to respond to these queries. This ensures that respondents are not led by pre-judgments or assumptions, and that managers do not merely convince themselves that their own prejudices are an accurate reflection of customer behavior or motivation.

This approach has gained credibility with the rise of the corporate anthropologist, whose broad remit is to gain an understanding of how, and for what purpose, customers actually utilize products and services, and how this is influenced by basic customer behaviors. This awareness is then applied to inform all aspects of the product cycle, from design and development to marketing. The use of such methodology is particularly prevalent in technology-based companies, where in three-quarters of cases the long and costly process of product development may be defeated by lack of a market. At Intel, anthropologist Genevieve Bell has undertaken extensive studies into the way technology products fit into the lives of ordinary consumers in markets as diverse as China and Western Europe, and she has observed that findings from research of this type raises serious questions about the suitability of the 'one world, one product' approach to marketing.[1]

While it may not be appropriate to make full-scale use of a corporate anthropologist, it can nevertheless be helpful to apply an informal ethnographic approach to understanding customer behavior. In the process of rooting out customer drivers, it is particularly useful to ask a version of these three questions. These questions will help the manager to understand the basis of customer motivation, beyond basic observations about what customers buy and how much they pay:-

- What are the customers doing with the product? How are they using it?
- What are the ultimate aims that the product or service is expected to achieve?
- What are the customers' comfort factors?

Comfort factors reflect those attributes that customers require of a product or service or its mode of supply in order to feel comfortable and confident in the purchase. These should be distinguished from options which may be attractive in themselves, but which are unlikely to prove advantageous in the absence of comfort factors.

Most important of all, spend time listening to the responses.

Tracking customer movements

The continuing development of global markets is having an impact on business at several levels. Not only are companies increasingly able to find customers in many different parts of the world, their manufacturing and supply bases are liable to shift to locations offering favorable conditions for inward investment, more competitive labor rates, better access to developing markets, or similar incentives. These shifts may involve direct relocation or expansion of manufacturing capacity, or they may extend procurement or the subcontracting of production to distant territories.

Whatever the case, shifts of this type affect almost all business-to-business sectors to some degree, and therefore may be of critical importance in assessing the potential of the global market. Established domestic customers who have moved into a different territory are likely to be more amenable to purchasing known products, provided they can rely on the levels of service and support to be expected in the domestic market. An awareness of current and ongoing customer movement is valuable to the development of an international strategy, as it provides an indication of where the organization might most easily and profitably seek to establish itself internationally.

Customer movements across territories occur for several, often closely related, reasons. These moves may be intended to equip the company with a degree of competitive advantage, perhaps in the form of lower overheads or geographical proximity to markets, thus leaving them better placed to serve their own new and existing customers more profitably than if they had retained a primarily domestic production base. These influences include the following:

- *Lower labor/production costs.* Many companies have taken the step of establishing manufacturing capacity or service facilities in developing economies with a lower cost base as a means of improving their own margins. This has been particularly well documented in labor intensive industries such as textiles.
- *Open new markets.* Companies in the process of opening up substantial new markets in a relatively distant part of the world often find practical benefit in situating a production facility in or near this territory. In this way, the organization benefits from both proximity to new markets and, in many cases, from the lower overheads that obtain in the very markets the company is endeavoring to penetrate.

- *Exploit sources of raw materials.* Industry sectors whose products are heavily dependent on specific raw materials for their manufacture have increasingly sought to realize the potential cost savings of relocating production closer to the source of the materials.
- *Investment incentives.* The process of globalization has led to fierce competition for foreign direct investment projects in almost every region of the world. Incentives for inward investment are generally open to all comers, but may be directed at particular sectors in an effort to create an industry cluster which, it is hoped, will spawn supporting industries, attain a critical mass of technological or research-based expertise, and attract even more foreign investment.

Of course, whatever circumstances drive a customer to move to or expand in a certain location can in the long run lose their comparative advantage, driving the customers to relocate production facilities yet again or, possibly, to turn away from the idea of a globalized production base altogether and rebuild production capacity in their domestic market.

Figure 4.3   Examples of Customer Movement

A recent, high profile example of the large-scale movement of business customers is the proliferation of call centers and software development centers in India, mainly serving customers in the United States and Europe. In this case comparatively low wages combined with a well-educated workforce with good English language skills has for many companies made the shift to the other side of the world worthwhile. In fact, in the field of software development this becomes a positive advantage, as the time difference allows Indian organizations to work 'overnight' to deliver solutions to Western clients at the beginning of their working day.

For an individual company the benefits in recognizing and responding to these movements can be enormous. A US-based company providing services to healthcare manufacturers in a range of territories had observed the attrition of its known customer base over a period of several years. The company had no idea what was causing this gradual but profound change in market structure, and was consequently unable to formulate a constructive response to it.

Viewed from a wider perspective, the problem became clear. In the early to mid 1990s medical product manufacturers from the US and Europe began to shift production capacity to territories in Southeast Asia. This was motivated primarily by the benefits of lower labor and production costs in the region, combined with the potential for accessing these newly developing markets. Additionally, companies manufacturing rubber-based products derived financial and logistic advantages from locating closer to the sources of their raw materials. Further research into the reasons for the shift suggested that it would continue, and would become a long-term feature of the industry.

With this framework in mind, the company accordingly moved into the new territories and set up facilities to service the growing healthcare industry in the region. Not only was the initial venture successful, but the company's enhanced awareness of the changing nature of its markets made it more alert to other potential opportunities in the region and beyond. Ultimately, the company has dominated the global market for its services.

In order to track these or any other type of customer movement it is essential to have an awareness of the industry and the market in which the potential customers operate, and to understand the considerations that they must take into account when making decisions about serving their own customer base.

Tracking customer movements internationally may also entail a more subtle assessment of outsourcing and procurement practices as they develop within industry sectors. To take one example, in Europe it is now relatively common in industries such as engineering for major manufacturers to outsource some or all aspects of component production to sub-contract firms in lower-cost economies, such as those in central and eastern Europe, while themselves retaining final assembly operations. This trend is also being pushed further down the line by smaller sub-contractors in developed markets who endeavor to enhance their price competitiveness by themselves sub-contracting to lower-cost producers in developing markets.

The first and most obvious effect of this trend is to reduce demand for engineering equipment in developed markets, causing the market to stagnate and causing suppliers to fight even more determinedly for both market share and adequate margins. Despite these difficulties, the market has not necessarily disappeared for good. In effect, a proportion of engineering production is shifting to new territories, driving a demand in these new locations for the machinery and equipment necessary to meet the quality requirements of world class manufacturers.

This type of customer tracking is challenging simply because such movements are not always highly visible or completely obvious. It may appear that production capacity is simply being reduced when in fact it has been relocated, either by means of direct customer movement or indirectly through a process of outsourcing.

Both types of customer movement, whether relocation or outsourcing, demand a corresponding identification and tracking of where and how purchasing decisions are being made. As companies expand and relocate throughout the global marketplace, responsibility for procurement may move accordingly for some items, while others remain under the central control of corporate headquarters. Outsourcing and sub-contracting do not necessarily make this procurement process any more straightforward: while many sub-contractors are free to equip themselves as they deem appropriate, some large manufacturers may require their contractors to purchase particular types of products or services, or products from specific manufacturers that are already known to conform to the requirements of the contracting company.

Customer tracking is a practical means of beginning to think about potential international markets. Assuming an awareness of the issues that influence customer behavior in the domestic market, and to which these companies must respond positively if they are to remain competitive, it is possible to develop a realistic sense of whether and how this customer base is moving its operations into new, global locations. This in turn may uncover opportunities for targeting markets at a later stage.

Tracking population shifts

In global consumer markets, the mirror image of corporate relocation is the potential for population movements across territories. A globalized economy also means globalized opportunities for work, education, leisure or, on a more basic level, refugee status. Even as individuals commit themselves to long-term or permanent residence in a foreign country, they often retain many of their established habits and tastes in food, clothing, entertainment, or other products or services that they are accustomed to accessing in their home territory. Population shifts may develop a critical mass in new regions or territories, signaling the potential for an internationalized niche market.

What initiates and sustains population movements large and homogeneous enough to generate a new consumer market in a foreign territory?

- *Immigration.* Immigration is perhaps the most visible means by which new consumer markets arise in territories where they did not exist before. The permanent migrant, economic or otherwise, has a history at least as old as that of colonialism, and in the face of wide disparities in global living standards and continuing instability in certain regions, the phenomenon shows no signs of disappearing.

  The impact of immigration in a national market may be seen clearly in the rise of the Hispanic population in the United States, particularly in areas of the country where such a population was not previously numerous. In the state of Iowa, an influx of Hispanic workers into communities with a predominantly northern European ancestry rapidly gave rise to a range of new markets for everything from hair oil to corn husks for wrapping enchiladas. A significant transnational population shift may also arise as a result of changing social expectations or practices. The attraction of a warmer and drier climate, combined with escalating house prices in the UK, has encouraged an increasing number of British nationals to invest in second or retirement homes in southern Europe, particularly in Spain. This has supported the development of estate agency and property management services aimed at these long-term expatriates.

- *Professional relocation.* Workers of all grades, whether highly paid professionals, those employed in craft skills such as construction, or simple manual laborers, may find advantages in temporarily transferring their labor to markets in which they stand to benefit either financially or personally from the move. Professional expatriation has long been a common part of making career progress within a diplomatic corps, a multinational corporation, or a transnational organization such as the United Nations. Expatriate employment may last for months or possibly years, and may operate on a highly individual basis. However, provided a relatively cohesive group of a significant size becomes established, and the individuals returning to their home country are regularly replaced by new expatriates to support the niche, a workable market may develop.

Although a shift in population may initially create a specialist niche within a wider territorial market, continuing growth in the size, wealth, or influence of this population may eventually result in niche products or services impacting on the mainstream market, either by becoming directly acceptable within the wider market or by influencing the development of new products aimed at the mass market.

The viability of a potential market niche created through population shifts may be tested by means of market assessment as described in Chapter 7, which addresses the process of assessing national markets, including changes in the demographic structure within a territory and the way in which this affects market development.

Building up an awareness of customer motivation is in itself a competitive advantage. Once the organization has an idea of what drives end-user behavior in the first instance, it will become possible to keep an eye on it either casually or through a process of formal monitoring. This will empower managers to track the direction of changes as they work through the market, to anticipate change as it develops, or even to instigate market change in a foreign territory by understanding how to identify and exploit customer drivers.

A sound awareness of customer motivation equips the international manager with enough information to ask intelligent questions when faced with unfamiliar situations, and to apply judgment to these situations in a constructive fashion. It also enables the manager to make rational sense of the random sales and business opportunities that arise unexpectedly, and to begin to examine them in a more critical light.

Note

1 The Industry Standard, May 14, 2001, Sharon Walsh (web edition)

5
Building a Foundation

The WRAP Stairway

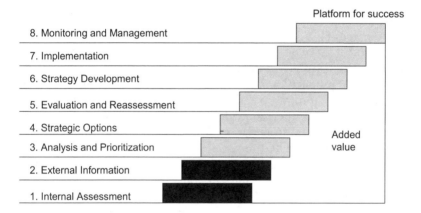

This chapter discusses the WRAP approach to corporate internal assessment and lays the foundations for targeting and selecting external information to be used in the information development element.

Too often strategy is regarded as some kind of purely external process, perhaps as a way of imposing the corporate will on the refractory world of customers and suppliers. The corporate vision and mission statements tend to read like promotions for apple pie (the best apple pie in the world, of course) made only from the world's finest apples, personally delivered, packaged with loving care and tenderness, and priced to the customer's satisfaction. Try reading the vision and mission statement of, for example, a retail bank and enjoy the dichotomy between these and the actual services provided. And that is no bad thing because operational strategy is used by boards of directors, or individual entrepreneurs, to achieve a different purpose. It is their job to strive to improve corporate prosperity, shareholder or legacy value, and the firm's prospects for survival and growth.

Essentially, corporate strategy is selfish, greedy and competitive because delivery of vision and mission requires the strategy to be corporately focused. Strategy objectives may be compiled with noble sentiments in mind; nevertheless they must reflect the realities of what needs to be achieved in order to develop prosperity and growth. To do so, these objectives are better formulated in the light of information and understanding of what may be achievable. In the international context this can be a much more complex set of tasks, as much information initially falls into the 'unknown' category. As information and awareness develop through the WRAP process, however, space is created for the evolution of strategic objectives.

Many established international corporations have already developed a deep understanding of the worlds they inhabit but this awareness seldom goes far beyond their particular business sector. What would happen, for example, if Halliburton, the US energy service giant, moved into consumer fashions? Or if Sony decided its future lay in agricultural production? Or McDonalds switched its focus to aircraft manufacture? Or Johnson and Johnson moved into computer games? The answer is that their strategies would require to be almost totally rebuilt from a fresh foundation of information and awareness. In considering the time and investment required to position these corporations where they are today, both the rewards and the costs of developing international business become apparent.

But the point of using WRAP, or any other rational strategy development process, is to reduce the time required and the costs involved in gaining information, exploiting awareness and implementing successful international strategies, in this case by using models to prioritize, target, build options and evaluate opportunities before implementation takes place. It can be thought of as a feasibility process.

Internal assessment

The process of internal assessment brings focus and discipline to the strategy development foundation. It means that subsequent decisions will be influenced by awareness of the reality of an organizational culture without sacrificing the competitive ambitions of the business. If an ambition is to become the undisputed world leader in a primary market sector, that's fine, as long as the company is prepared to resource that ambition. But before this step is taken, simple intelligence demands that an attempt is made to comprehend the company's own internal strengths and position.

The point of this initial internal assessment is not to nail down an irrevocable set of conditions under which the organization will be forced to operate during the process of strategy development. Instead, it is useful to think in terms of outlining a realistic picture of the business as it currently functions and the resources that might actually be available for future programs. Understanding the current state of the organization leads to more sensible judgments about what is feasible and what is ultimately impractical in terms of what the organization is capable of achieving.

Available resources

The question of resources is fundamentally about the existing infrastructure of the organization and what level and type of development it can support in the medium to long term. What does the company have to work with now, and where will it need to develop or acquire new resources?

Market perceptions

In the first instance, most organizations operate within a corporate culture that is moderately well understood and accepted by its own staff. Defining that culture, however, is an activity that tends to be rarely undertaken unless the company is subject to some kind of internal review, and thus the internal perception of the company can often be different from its perception by others outside. Simply gaining an awareness of the 'known' elements as they will be perceived by potential customers and influence international business development can be an enlightening experience, but represents the start point for any change or adjustment that may be required.

For example, a small food processing firm in Egypt sought to develop contracts to supply American military forces located within the territory and was surprised when its offer was rejected, not on cost grounds but on the basis of lack of confidence by the potential customers in its hygiene arrangements. The reason for this surprise was that the company believed it operated to western standards of hygiene; although it is fair to say that it was a pretty clean operation compared to many of its Egyptian competitors, the difference between its own perception and the actuality of standards required of western food processing plants was wide, and was unlikely to be bridged in the short to medium term. In a similar vein, many managers in the UK would perceive the manufacturing plants in the national engineering industry as being well equipped and efficiently operated. Ask a South Korean about British plants and the answer comes back 'aha – factories with wooden floors!'.

To slightly misquote Robert Burns, the famous Scottish poet, 'Oh, would the Lord the gift give us, to see ourselves as others see us.' It is important, in viewing one's own organization, not only to be honest in assessment of strengths and weaknesses, skills and attributes, but also to try to relate these to external, foreign experience so that pointers can be laid to potential aspects for change. It is not suggested that at this point there should be a wholesale clearout of current corporate culture, simply that these issues should be addressed and noted so that change, when required, can be understood and appropriately implemented.

Corporate culture

If you listen carefully to the directors' views of an organization that certainly some of them will have worked their way through for many years, there exists a significant element of a corporate culture which hopefully contributes to the success of the firm but also reflects a perception of an organizational culture as the directors like it to be. Operational managers, on the other hand, tend to view the corporate culture as a series of positives or negatives rather than a balanced corporate entity. All this can be very interesting and corporate psychologists have been known to spend entire careers nosing around these issues, but for the purposes of the WRAP process it is sufficient to be aware of what bureaucrats might call the broad thrust, or dynamics of the corporation. It is critical that the key issues of the corporate culture are understood, and these are likely to become evident from general discussion with directors and senior managers, both as groups and as individuals. These critical issues might typically include:-

- Is the organization outward or inward looking? Is it a listening or a pushing organization?
- Is the company traditionally receptive to new ideas, or does it fear change?
- Is there awareness of the existence and validity of foreign business cultures, or a preference to replicate itself overseas?
- Is the company prepared to take risks in its domestic market to achieve gain and growth in foreign markets?

- Are the key people in the organization internationally minded, or do they tend to take domestic cultures abroad? For example, is there some resentment of the lunchtime siesta common in many countries with hot climates, because the existing work pattern has to be adapted to it?

- And are the senior managers as attuned to international development as the directors or do they see this corporate ambition as unfeasible or a distraction from the domestic business?

There are many questions that can and should be asked, preferably by an independent person without the corporate baggage of historical relationships with colleagues and the company, so that indications of corporate culture can be identified with some degree of credibility and potential for motivating change as required.

The other critical aspect in identifying how a company, rather than an individual, thinks and operates is in the nature of its business and current relationships with customers and suppliers. One of the most evident examples is in the defense industry where medium to large firms, in particular, have a strong relationship with their national and possibly international ministries of defense, and whose executives are often drawn from the ranks of former serving officers. The nature of the defense business, particularly for prime contractors, can be broadly characterized as a series of related contracts, often long term, influenced by relationships with contacts in the procurement offices, which are also moderately long term. Such companies are also likely to have a track record of successfully completing previous contracts of a similar type. Because development contracts for major weapons systems may be placed five, ten or twenty years ahead of expected delivery, and new technologies that come along in the meantime are sometimes required to be absorbed in the development program, this tends to create a commercially comfortable situation with most stress arising in the technical and developmental operations. On the other hand, governments have been known to change, delay or cancel both large and small programs for economic or political reasons, and this represents the critical risk for defense companies as their dependency on a single customer, the government, is pretty well total.

The largely risk averse nature of such a corporate culture needs to be taken into account as soon as a defense (or other government supply) company seeks to extend its markets internationally, and the same is true for firms that are more commercially aware. Going outside the comfort zone is always a challenging experience; the critical issue is how much attitudes need to change to successfully address new challenges.

Management resources

Management resources are an often neglected aspect of international strategic development. Anyone who has whiled away their time in airport departure lounges and hotel rooms can attest to the fact that business travel itself is time consuming, not to mention the preparatory work that must be done before anyone leaves the office. There needs to be a clear managerial responsibility for international business development, and if tasks are to be split between several staff members there should nevertheless be an individual with the authority to make decisions and the ability to keep the project on track to ensure that it does not lose momentum and melt away.

Given the fact that much non-operational capacity – or fat – has been trimmed away over the past decade, it's also necessary to recognize that time spent on international development is in many cases likely to conflict with the management of domestic business priorities. Unless the organization already has specialist staff, or the financial resources are available to take them on, a certain amount of overlap is unavoidable. It must be clear from the outset how any potential conflict will be managed and where staff priorities lie, while at the same time allowing sufficient management effort to be directed towards international development. Without such controls there is a risk that both domestic and international programs will collapse into a welter of conflicting priorities and initiatives.

However, much of this required commitment will evolve during the course of the development process, and indeed any evident and potentially valuable internal resources (such as people with foreign language capability or who have previous relevant experience in target territories) may influence the course of strategic development by utilizing known strengths as a part of the targeting process.

Equally important is the experience of the managers involved, which will influence how ambitious a company can afford to be in selecting and pursuing market opportunities. At this point it may be useful to repeat the vital distinction between export and international business. Understanding export regulations and dealing with the necessary documentation is essential, but it is fundamentally an administrative issue. International business development is a strategic and management issue and needs to be approached with a view to the longer term positioning of the organization in global markets.

Operational resources

It is critical to understand the operational resources that can be brought into play in response to the development process. As and when a range of development options have been identified, how effectively can new customers be serviced? Furthermore, how capable is the operational side of the organization of absorbing any changes that may be necessitated by market expansion?

Naturally, relevant operational issues will vary according to the nature of the enterprise. For a manufacturing-focused enterprise, production capacity is clearly the resource on which all else depends. What can't be made won't be sold, broadly speaking, although again the evolution of a strategy may offer alternative options or ways forward. For example, on a sales trip to Asia an IT systems company was offered the opportunity to convert its programs to operate using Oracle, a far better platform for international markets than the original bespoke model used. The price was low, the sales opportunity available thereafter was immense, and the offer was made by one of India's largest corporations. As it turned out, the company was too slow in considering the opportunity and ultimately sold out to a European firm whose first move was to convert to an Oracle platform and successfully address new regional markets.

Furthermore, be clear about the nature of existing productive capacity. Know what can be made now, and what else might be feasible (or not) in future. This issue extends to the organization's experience in utilizing subcontract services for key elements of the production process. It is commonplace in contemporary supply chains to either be a sub-contractor, to use them, or possibly both simultaneously. How comfortable is the company with putting processes out to contract? Thinking ahead, it may become practical to make use of contractors or suppliers in other territories as a means of obtaining financial or other competitive advantages.

A broad understanding of the technical resources at a company's disposal gives an indication of the kind of market development the organization can sustain. How far is it possible for the organization to adapt to the demands of an unfamiliar market while continuing to meet the requirements of existing ones? This may well become an issue when it is discovered that the global market requires something slightly or perhaps entirely different from the existing product or service range.

This is essentially a two-part question. First of all, it is an issue of how far the company is willing and able to go to accommodate the potential requirements of new and different customers. Strictly speaking this may be less of a technical problem than a marketing one, but it is at least partially dependent on the company's ability to support what may amount to significant changes in its product offering. In this context, design and presentation really do function as an adjunct to R&D capabilities. Not only must the products be fit for the purpose, they need to look the part in a foreign context, and it is up to the company to decide how much of a product revamp could be sustained in order to extend the worldwide customer base.

Secondly, technical resourcing is also an issue of how the organization might be positioned in the global marketplace. This question hinges primarily on research and development capabilities and the organization's ability to translate these into marketable products. Again, this is not the moment to exaggerate the innovative or entrepreneurial orientation of the company. Truly cutting-edge products require markets able to utilize and appreciate them, while less technically robust products need to locate themselves in a competitive framework suitable to their level of development. Looking further ahead, any future decisions about strategic alliances and partnerships may well be influenced by the technical expertise resident in the organization, compared to that necessary to compete effectively in global markets.

Financial resources

Of course nobody would deliberately spend more on market development than they could hope to get back in profits. Would they? In our experience, one of the most serious problems for firms trying to develop international presence stems from neglecting to balance expenditure against opportunity. Perfectly respectable concepts such as 'opportunity cost' and 'testing the market' are often used as phrases to cover up actual unbudgeted expenditure blown away in a plethora of ill-thought-out promotional schemes involving international travel. It has to be accepted that international business development, as with any other venture, takes time and costs money. How long it takes, how much it costs, and the likely levels of return patently depend on specific circumstances, but in any event it makes little sense to embark on a development program that the organization is ultimately unwilling to resource properly. Ways of gaining guidance on potential cost vary but could include:-

• How much did it cost to open up current international markets?

Figure 5.1   Confusing the Issue

A small American firm that manufactured a specialist product sold primarily to engineering plants started its international business development by exporting to the UK, and eventually developed a manufacturing capability in the UK through sub-contracting to an even smaller company. As the business found itself competing in an increasingly competitive and price-sensitive market, it was decided that the best way to maintain profitability was to increase the volume sales of its products, and continental Europe was selected as the most obvious target. This territory, of course, contains many major manufacturing countries including Germany, Italy, France and Spain, so the rationale for this development was that between them, these countries may be able to sustain sales at the UK level.

Two issues immediately arose, the first being that following some simple research, it was discovered that Germany alone could absorb four or five times the sales levels in the UK. The second issue was that the manufacturing sub-contractor did not have the capacity to expand production levels. No German distributor was identified as willing to constrain sales at the necessary low level, nor was the sub-contractor prepared to invest further. And the American parent was unwilling to bear the cost of borrowing to increase the firm's US capacity, which ran the risk of reducing the profitability of the company.

This conundrum was only resolved several years later when the company sold out to a larger competitor that was able to manufacture and ship all the products needed for both its domestic and European markets from its facility in America. The price for the company, which was effectively forced into the sale by its rapidly diminishing return, was much lower than the directors could have expected had they had a real European customer base to promote.

- Are budgetary priorities within the domestic organization a useful guide?
- What level of product profitability is required to cover the cost of international sales?

At this stage it is not important, nor indeed is it necessarily desirable, to produce a detailed budget relating to international business development. It is much more useful to have a broad range of figures in mind against which opportunities can be assessed as they unfold during strategy development; later on, when solid and profitable opportunities have been identified, it will be appropriate to delineate a budget that takes account of specific courses of action.

Current products

So just what is it the company makes, does, and sells? This covers not only the range and features of existing products and services, but also any supporting services accompanying the product range and the way they are currently provided. Furthermore, it is necessary to have a clear understanding of the existing cost structure and the corresponding levels of pricing and profitability that are being sought in the international venture. Setting realistic pricing levels is dependent on the nature and context of the target market, and may well become a feature that figures high on the criteria to be adopted in determining priority markets. Logistics and after-sales support and service will also need to be factored into the process of participating in a foreign market. Not only will these necessities incur a cost, they may also have implications for existing operational and technical procedures on a corporate basis.

Competitive environment

Every business has a native environment, and almost inevitably it's a highly competitive one. One of the great myths of international business is that of the Empty Market: the land that few or no competitors have discovered, awash with potential customers who are only just beginning to understand their burning need for overshoes made from hard wearing resins. Seriously, market opportunities a little like this sometimes do arise, but they don't last long, mainly because they've also been spotted by aggressive competitors from Germany, China, Brazil, the US, and Thailand, all of whom will conspire to help the market regain its competitive status. Indeed, if a national market appears to offer a landscape comparatively free from significant competition, it is worth asking why this situation has arisen. It may indicate that the organization has actually identified at an early stage that the market could be responsive to development. It could equally suggest that potential competitors have already spotted the fact that there is likely, in practice, to be very little worth competing for.

For this reason if no other it is important to be familiar with existing competitors, because wherever in the world the organization chooses to operate it is likely to come up against a similar range of companies. It is likely that experience in the domestic market already provides an indication of who the competitors are and what they are offering their customer base. It is also helpful at this point to find out where else in the world existing competitors are active. This doesn't imply any plan to blindly follow them wherever they go. For example, it's useful to be aware that they are currently more active in certain parts of the world rather than others, and there may be good reasons for this that only become clear at a later stage.

When defining the competition, it is crucial to be clear about the source of competition and its effect on the organization's own product or service base. In other words, competitors may include not only companies offering very similar and directly competitive products; the competitor base may additionally encompass those firms that serve the needs and desires of the same customers by a different route. By neglecting this aspect of competition, the Polaroid Corporation found itself in trouble through failing to acknowledge quickly enough the speed at which digital imaging technologies, essentially competitive to their own products, would grow. But it is not just new, high-tech products that pose such a threat. In some developing markets in particular, low-tech competitors that may not be seen at all in the domestic market can pose a significant challenge due to their responsiveness to customer concerns about such issues as pricing, or long-term product maintenance.

Although we have devoted an entire chapter to understanding the behavior of international customers, the necessary prelude to this is ensuring that there is a reasonable awareness of the behavior and requirements of existing customers. Sketch out a profile of the customer base: who they are, what they buy and why. Is the market cyclical? Is it growing or declining? Has it undergone any significant shifts or changes recently? Global markets may not replicate the patterns familiar from the domestic market, but having something concrete to look for will be of assistance in spotting analogous trends in other territories.

Corporate background

This addresses collective corporate experience in the field of international business. Where does the organization stand right now, what are the consequences for global corporate ambitions?

As always, honesty is the best policy. If the organization is already operating successfully in one or more foreign markets, what insights can be drawn from this experience? Anyone with all the answers is probably not reading this book, so we will move on to those people who have perhaps struck lucky in isolating a stray opportunity and developing it further. It may be useful to work through this issue by utilizing the points outlined above as a basis for identifying where and how the organization has been most responsive to market requirements.

If on the other hand the organization has already had a painful and costly experience in foreign enterprise, or if these efforts towards global expansion have brought only mediocre or no profitability, now is the time to resurrect that experience and examine it for flaws. For example, how were target markets identified, and what approach to the market was taken? What unexpected difficulties materialized during the development process? Think not just about the obvious reason for poor performance; try to get at the underlying problem. If this proves impossible, all is not lost. The application of strategic thinking to the next venture is intended to illuminate these pitfalls before managers innocently wander into them all over again.

If this is a first attempt at developing an international presence, be upfront about corporate concerns. Are there situations or potential problems that the management is actively trying to avoid, or which provoke particular concern in the organization? These may include, for example, issues around the management of distant business relationships. Or is it simply the case that lack of experience is operating to curtail global ambitions? These concerns are reasonable. Only a fool would stride boldly into a dark room without even a box of matches for company. Of course, inexperience can be remedied by falling into holes in the dark, but it can also be upgraded rather less painfully through the development and use of information and awareness.

What should emerge from this moment of corporate introspection is an appreciation of what the company can and does do well, what it is capable of doing, and what it does not do well or prefers to avoid doing altogether. Internal assessment should provide a snapshot of the organization that should be, either literally or figuratively, borne in the mind of the strategist while working through the strategy development process. It is also useful to note at this stage roughly how flexible the internal attributes of the organization really are. How much scope is there to alter any or all aspects of the current orientation of the company, either in a psychological sense or in terms of accessing adequate resources to effect such a change? Is some degree of change feasible, or is the organization so conservative that it will have great difficulty sustaining substantial changes to existing practice?

At this point these questions do not require hard and fast answers. Rather, they should offer the strategist some sense of the internal flexibility of the organization and how adaptable it will be in the face of challenges in a global business environment. This will become particularly significant in Chapter 9, in which the process of strategy development is brought to its culmination, and where substantive changes in some aspect of corporate business practice may become key to successful strategy development.

External information: establishing the search

Creating strategic objectives

At the outset of the strategy development process, the creation of strategic objectives operates to focus the attention of the management on the purpose of strategy by defining what the strategy is expected to achieve. Strategic objectives should be consistent with corporate objectives but should not be confused with them.

Corporate objectives, including the organization's mission and vision statements, relate to the purpose of the organization, while strategic objectives are aimed at identifying ways to achieve these corporate objectives. The latter act as guides to the strategy development process, ensuring that decisions made and activities undertaken are truly responsive to corporate goals and not merely erratic reactions to disparate pieces of information.

The other important caveat is that strategic objectives, like many other elements of the WRAP process, are not necessarily set in stone. They can change as and when the organization becomes cognisant that such change may be necessary or beneficial. For example, the information development phase may indicate that the organization is already a market leader in key territories. In this case, the strategic objective may reasonably alter from 'becoming a market leader' to 'expanding into new territories with potential for growth'.

The appropriate level of detail required in a company's initial international strategy objectives depends on how the company is currently positioned in the development of its international business and what level of corporate international awareness exists. A newcomer with little experience would be well advised to keep the objectives simple, perhaps seeking to focus on a single foreign country or global region and to gain sales equivalent to perhaps 20 per cent of domestic sales within three years of market entry. Another firm already established as a significant international player might focus objectives on gaining some percentage market share of a world market, differentiated between product ranges. The difference isn't actually the complexity but rather the level of awareness of each entity, and thus the ability to judge possibilities within a known and understood commercial environment.

The reason for having objectives may seem self-evident: they provide focus, take account of corporate capabilities and resources, allow plans to be developed, and offer a means of measuring success. It is nevertheless surprising how many firms seek to develop business internationally with no specific objective in mind other than to utilize spare domestic capacity, to increase sales in general or to exploit a specific, transient opportunity that has been brought to their attention. While all of these are perfectly acceptable ways of operating, they are based on simple opportunism rather than planned or WRAPped opportunism and often lead to disappointing results and far higher costs than the more rational and deliberate approach advocated here.

Figure 5.2 US Defense Market

We can compare the approach adopted by two British firms that sought to enter the US defense market by winning prime contracts with the US Department of Defense. Company A was an engineering firm that specialized in manufacturing certain types of naval equipment, while Company B was involved in commercial aircraft engine overhaul. Both had experience in working with the UK Ministry of Defense, but of course the procurement systems operated by the US military is entirely different from most others.

Company A spent nearly ten years and invested many millions of dollars in following up what it saw as bidding opportunities for its skills, usually brought to its attention through the US official contract publication, *Commerce Business Daily*, but sometimes introduced by British defense attaches in the US. With the help of specialists, Company B examined the US military market for aircraft engine overhaul contracts, visited the military establishments where engines were being overhauled both to learn more about the processes adopted and to introduce the company, and targeted specific contracts as well as identifying the likely timing of their potential procurement. The company made sure it was on the bidders' list for each contract, thus gaining access to pre-contract briefing sessions, and finally gained a contract about three years after it started on this process. The total investment was around half a million dollars.

The benefits gained by adopting a more structured approach to identifying and seizing an opportunity is evident here. It is more reliable and less reliant on chance.

There are, of course, many other factors that can influence the initial creation of these 'wish' objectives, not least those elements that have determined a company's progress in its current markets. Larger organizations often build a portfolio of operating divisions or subsidiaries among which there are likely to be star performers as well as poor performers, whether measured by return on investment, return on sales, sector market share, cash flow contribution, or any other measure, and it is reasonable to assume that these firms are seeking a balance between divisions that are in the early stages of development and others that are going through the matured 'cash cow' phase. As most of these corporations also have public company status through stock exchange quotation, maintenance and improvement in share values often becomes an absolute priority. The pursuit of balanced and measurable strategies for international development can thus be considered as a critical process. Unless the company is in the oil production business, in which case it all becomes much simpler and dependent on flow rates, oil drilling down time and the international oil price.

Smaller firms do not generally need to address all of these issues and are most dependent on the level and value of sales, and costs of production. International business offers a natural extension to income, or a reduction in cost of production, one way or another, and their initial objectives tend to be focused accordingly.

Parameters and criteria

In the WRAP process, parameters and criteria are the means of defining the preferred scope of the strategy by first of all narrowing the focus of strategy development, and secondly by preparing the ground for manageable information development. Like strategic objectives, parameters and criteria may be initially defined and subsequently changed to take account of new information or a change in corporate perspective. This marks the beginning of the prioritization process.

The first step in prioritization is the definition of parameters. In this context, a parameter is defined as a line that is drawn that determines the limit of an area of interest. In effect, parameter identification seeks out one or two basic, essential characteristics that a national market must display in order to be considered a high priority: lacking such characteristics, the territory will in the first instance be regarded as a low priority, or possibly as unsuitable for any further development. Definition of parameters works to bring some territories to the foreground and relegate others, as a means of narrowing the scope of enquiry to a more manageable field.

There are two principal means by which parameters can be defined. The first is geographic. This has particular relevance in global markets, as an organization may be aware from the outset that strategic development of east Asian markets is a critical corporate priority, and therefore energies must of necessity be focused on this region alone. Geographic parameters are essentially simple, defining which national markets are included in the regional scope of enquiry and which are not.

The second method of defining parameters relates directly to essential market characteristics. These may be technological, developmental, financial, or something else, but they define a critical aspect of the territory that makes some level of market entry realistic, as described in Figure 5.3. Essentially the parameter represents the outer limit of markets of interest, beyond which the rest of the world can for the time being be left dark. Defining parameters of this type become particularly important when the organization has determined upon a global remit for strategy development: this provides the only method of paring down the territories under examination so that information development becomes a more manageable task. Parameter definition of this type may exclude many territories, or it may exclude almost none.

Figure 5.3   Potential Parameters

A firm that specializes in supplying the nuclear power generation sector would only have an interest in reviewing territories where nuclear power stations exist or are in course of development. It would simply be a waste of time and resource to look at any other countries. A company located in the Middle East that manufactures computer systems with Arabic software may prefer its initial exposure to international markets to be focused entirely on Arabic speaking territories, or on other Muslim territories where the Koran is in daily use. On the other hand, someone supplying powered wheelchairs for the disabled, which are saleable in many parts of the world, might draw its parameter at countries with a relatively high GDP per head, thus indicating the potential for personal financial capacity to purchase the chairs at relatively high prices. Parameters can therefore be perceived as delineating the world for which the strategies are to be developed, and can encompass an entirely global or determinedly partial reach.

For parameters of the second category it is likely that some degree of research may be needed in order to accurately identify territories that conform to the required definition. Although prejudice of one kind or another can play a part in selecting parameters, it is more useful if the selection process is driven by a degree of information. In practice, this may be made available by government departments, trade associations, chambers of commerce or other trade bodies. Comparison with competitors' international ventures can also be a factor particularly when the competitive benefits they gain become publicly evident. China provides a good example of this development. Following President Nixon's famous visit to China the Chinese market began to open up, but it was a very slow beginning in which accepted lore was that firms had to spend years working with the Chinese before there could be any hope of making a profit. Now, although there are still difficulties, China has the fastest growth among all the world's major markets, both in terms of consumption and production of goods and services. In the early days China was normally excluded from review as companies often felt they had neither the time nor the resources to develop the market. Now, the country is probably the single key focus – or single geographic parameter – for the attention of firms involved in international business although it can still be a risky market for many small firms that lack the resource to work successfully over time with Chinese partners.

In general it is reasonably simple to draw geographic parameters within which appropriate criteria can be applied, markets sought and strategies developed that will maximize benefit to companies. Technology parameters, however, are often drawn to reflect a company's skills and background, but fail to reflect changes in market demand or new and competing technological developments. As observed in a previous chapter the Polaroid Corporation found itself in trouble through failing to acknowledge quickly enough the speed at which digital imaging technologies, essentially competitive to their own products, would grow. It is worth considering this parameter, when reviewing a strategy development process, in the light of a definition of what business a company is actually in. There are many other books available that address this issue at length; suffice to say that taking strategic account of competition and competitors often requires thought to be applied to defining the competition. If there are alternative approaches to achieving the same outcome as that achieved by an organization's product, then it is useful for a strategy to encompass the threats potentially posed by these technologies and to the other opportunities that they may present.

In considering technological parameters, the strategist should at this point endeavor to keep the necessity for research to a minimum in order to avoid becoming bogged down in a complex task of information development. In choosing second-category parameters, the strategist should focus on information that is simple, easily identified, and easy to access. Two rules aid in this type of parameter definition:

• Parameter identification should rely on reasonably precise data. Does a market display a particular characteristic, or is it absent? For best results, a parameter may best be defined through utilization of a yes/no question offering a clear answer, or through quantitative data that allows direct comparisons and clear prioritization.
• Avoid parameters requiring qualitative data. Qualitative information is necessarily subject to interpretation and hedged about with caveats, and for this reason is unlikely to offer clear guidance as to which territories are truly appropriate for further analysis at an early stage.

Definition of criteria is the second step in the prioritization process. Criteria are market characteristics that will be used to provide the measures for prioritizing or ranking markets or opportunities. Definitions of criteria respond to an organization's requirements of a market in order to meet strategic objectives as they have been identified to this point. These can be as complex as the company wishes; complexity, however, tends to create more severe constraints on the identification of areas of interest, as do criteria based on the requirement of very precise data, and can lead to failure in spotting opportunities because lines are drawn too sharply. Preferred criteria should generally be

Figure 5.4   Losing the Opportunity

A German manufacturer of electromedical equipment was well established in its European markets, and expanded slowly by applying as its key criterion a requirement that a national market must be able to absorb at least 40 of its machines per year. During a large healthcare exhibition in Hanover, Germany, a medical equipment distributor from Spain came onto the firm's stand and offered his company's services in Spain, as he'd noticed that the German company was not represented there.

The Germans had not previously considered Spain as a market territory as they assumed that the country could not sustain its 40 machine sales requirement, but nevertheless were persuaded that there may be an opportunity worth the risk. The Spanish distributor was taken on and in his first full year sold 3 machines. During the somewhat rancorous meeting that followed the Germans dismissed the distributor, who promptly went to another manufacturer and agreed to represent them in Spain.

Within two years he was selling over 50 machines per year. The Germans were horrified at their mistake and it took many years for them to reach their original criterion of 40 Spanish machine sales, as their competitors had by now reached almost market dominance. The situation had arisen because the company selected a criterion that put rigid limitations on its willingness to consider new markets, thus in practice ensuring that they would only consider entering mature and highly competitive markets.

broadly based because markets and opportunities change and because information on these changes is often both late and imprecise.

There can also be as many criteria as seem appropriate, bearing in mind that each one adds another ranking measure and thus makes analysis of results more complex. This can, however, be overcome by determining and ranking the importance of each criterion in its own right, so that once the key criteria have been met and priorities established, the others can be used as refining tools.

Criteria are intended to function as a reflection of the organization's understanding of the customer or client base and the markets in which these operate. This is in direct contrast to the approach of some firms that would classify themselves, or be known by others, as 'product-pushers', by which it is meant that they will sell their products to anyone, anywhere, at any time. The only criteria in this case is whether they can achieve volume sales comparatively rapidly, without any extended enquiry into the nature of customer demand. It's a hit and miss business predicated on a numbers game. On the other hand, a company that can recognize its customer segment can not only organize itself to service that segment but can also manage its own corporate and market development. Developing and addressing criteria for prioritizing targets is a part of that management process that can be reviewed and revisited to take account of changing circumstances, ensuring that the organization is not caught out by unexpected failures of demand.

This process may be best demonstrated by working through a wholly imaginary example of an organization getting to grips with strategic issues in the global healthcare market. Healthcare may seem to be an unusual choice in these circumstances, given the fact that the structure, provision and funding of healthcare varies so significantly across territories; however, this very fact forces us, and our putative organization, to confront a range of issues arising directly from the huge variation in market conditions that will be encountered globally.

Let us look more closely at our imaginary company, Smith and Co., based near Boston in the USA. The organization is a manufacturer of electrodiagnostic devices for home healthcare, including a cardiac monitor for use in the home as a means for individuals to keep tabs on their heart rate and to allow them to alert a doctor if they are concerned about any anomalies. For the purposes of global expansion, the organization has decided to focus on the cardiac monitor as the product that is most likely to find an international market. Annual turnover is on the order of US$60 million: 70 per cent of sales come from the US market, 20 per cent from Europe, and 10 per cent from the rest of the world.

The initial internal assessment outlines the current state of the organization. In terms of market perception, the company provides home healthcare devices that are not considered to be at the cutting edge of medical technology, but are nevertheless sound and reliable devices to alert individuals to potential health problems before they become catastrophic. Let us assume the company is quoted on NASDAQ; despite its avowedly entrepreneurial outlook, the chief officers are in practice quite conservative in global terms, particularly given the fact that they are unfamiliar with foreign markets and lack the means of evaluating them adequately.

The firm possesses a Vice President, Business Development overseeing sales and marketing activity. Working under her is an International Sales Manager handling all non-US promotional activity. The firm would be willing to consider additional staff operating in key regions, provided the investment could be justified by an anticipated increase in returns. Funds are available for this and for market development, but their release will be dependent on making a case for enhanced investment.

Smith and Co. manufacture and assembles its devices in the US, utilizing some components produced by a subcontractor in Taiwan. The company has spare capacity due to the highly competitive market conditions in their domestic territory. Although the products are healthcare devices, they are intended for use in the home and are therefore driven primarily by consumer demand influenced by health issues. The devices are sold mainly through distributors, who then sell the products through catalogues or retail outlets. The cardiac monitors retail for $250–$300.

The US market for home healthcare devices is maturing, with a number of US competitors present in the market. There are also significant competitors from Germany and Switzerland, and a range of smaller competitors from other countries make up the rest of the market. In Europe, Smith and Co. currently have a presence through distributors in the UK, the Netherlands, Sweden (covering Norway, Finland, and Eastern Europe), Germany (covering Austria and German-speaking Switzerland), and France (covering French-speaking Belgium and Switzerland).

Smith and Co.'s principal strategic objective is increased turnover and profitability in key European markets. This operates as a means of reducing exposure to the US market, which is highly competitive and price sensitive. It would also serve the purpose of absorbing spare manufacturing capacity in the US facility.

The parameters of the strategy development program are, in this case, straightforward geographic parameters. They encompass Western Europe, including both territories in which the organization has a presence and those in which it has never sold products. The parameters exclude EU accession territories. Existing experience in a variety of markets suggests to the management that European territories are most likely to possess both the developed consumer markets and necessary pricing levels to maintain profitability. Other markets that may offer appropriate pricing levels, such as the Middle East or certain territories in East Asia, are deemed to be less acceptable on the basis that they are almost entirely unfamiliar to the management; their distance from headquarters also indicates a premium to be invested in management time and development expenses, such as travel.

Having defined the objectives and parameters for their venture, and having outlined a succinct description of the present state of the organization, Smith and Co. need now to consider which criteria are appropriate to their strategic objectives. The market criteria deemed to be most relevant under the circumstances include:-

- Significant home health care device market
- Pricing for comparable products at the same or higher levels than the US

- Market growth potential
- Established distributor network
- Some presence of competitive products

Criteria are in practice market-led. That is, territories are being sought that are likely to provide markets that will function as the best match for the stated criteria. The highest strategic priority will be given to those markets that match the criteria most closely, because they should offer the company the best opportunity for market development, whether or not the company is already established in these markets. Therefore, determination of the criteria requires the most careful consideration.

The next issue for the organization is ranking these six criteria in a way that can allow for targeting the priority market or markets, and that means deciding which criteria are critical to the potential success of the venture. Smith and Co. has a challenge that can take several routes. Pricing is an evident issue, but how would a potential 300 high-value unit sales in a small market compare to 3000 lower-value unit sales in a larger market that may offer greater long-term prospects for development?

In our view, because there are several criteria available with which to qualify the choice of market, it makes more sense to move from apparently large markets, offering greater overall potential for sales, to the smaller markets, which offer less scope for future development but in which other criteria come more evidently into play. The dichotomy here is simple: other things being equal, the organization is likely to need to invest similar sums in developing one European market (or any other regional market) as compared to another in terms of the expected return.

Here, we return in a sense to our Peruvian dilemma from Chapter 1. In this case the Peruvian market was deemed highly accessible and even friendly; what no-one initially took into account was the potential of an even greater return to be derived from investing wisely in a larger, if more difficult, territory. Larger territories may indeed be more difficult of access, but the returns they are capable of generating may be far larger than those of a small, easily handled market. Furthermore, even a small, low-level presence in a large market is capable of being extended as the participant become familiar with the territory and gains confidence and contacts. By contrast, a big fish in a small pond has to stay put.

Management time and traveling and research expenses, including time spent developing presence in prioritized markets, will need to be invested in any case, and this investment does not come cheap. From our perspective it makes most sense to initially identify the size of potential markets, rank them in order, and then examine the fit of these markets against the criteria. In practice it may turn out that the largest markets provide an unsuitable platform for meeting the company's strategic objectives.

However, once the organization is aware of this it can avoid wasting investment in these territories and focus on those markets in which it is most likely to find the necessary returns in an environment that does not pose insuperable problems of access.

For Smith and Co. the most rational ranking for these criteria in order to deliver territorial markets in order of priority would be:-

1. Size of home health care market
2. Available pricing levels
3. Presence of competitive products. Pioneering is expensive and in most circumstances is best left to those with the deepest pockets
4. Market growth potential
5. Established distributor network

The parameters and criteria thus established provide a solid platform from which the company can establish its priority target markets that take full account of its objectives and its resources. This means that the company can have confidence that its strategic development program is likely to identify the key markets to which it can sensibly devote its resources and reduce or eliminate the risk of waste at this early stage in terms of time, effort and finance.

6

Information Development

The WRAP Stairway

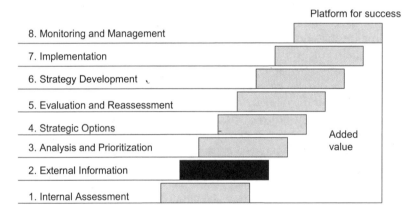

This chapter focuses on the acquisition and use of external information for guiding market prioritization and strategy development.

The classics of strategy, whether they emanate from eastern or western traditions, are united in their emphasis on two crucial aspects of strategic development: the vital importance of external information, and the necessity of utilizing critical analysis to make profitable judgments based on this information. Their impact seems to be mitigated, however, by an important corollary accepting that not everything can be known as and when it's required, and therefore the strategist must be prepared to operate on the basis of partial or incomplete knowledge.

Even in modern literature on management, it's difficult to find such a succinct description of a real-world dilemma. So far we have gone to great lengths to emphasize the importance of knowledge and awareness, only to end up acknowledging that this approach has its limitations and can never be complete. To make matters worse, the concept of the dynamic marketplace suggests that the world changes even as we sit and think about it. How in that case is it possible to make informed decisions that have a basis in reality?

This is not really the paradox it seems to be at first glance. Practical action does not require an encyclopedic knowledge of all possible sets of circumstances. Rather, it depends on an informed awareness of the background against which the individual or organization operates, as well as an understanding of the implications that this environment has for real world operations.

The quality of the information at the manager's command is far more important than its sheer quantity. This suggests that it is valuable to know what sort of information is likely to be required and to ensure insofar as possible that it is consistent. This permits a sharper focus on critical issues and correspondingly reduces the amount of time spent wading through no doubt interesting but potentially superfluous data. It also helps in avoiding the information overload that can afflict modern business by paralyzing decision making through an oversupply of data and a surfeit of analysis that may or may not be sound.

Assessment of the market or territory is usually built on basic market research, but when utilized effectively this encompasses much more than a straightforward comparison of market size followed by an estimate of the putative market share to be gained. It also contains a vital element of judgment, which finds its basis in the corporate objectives identified in the previous phase of the WRAP process. The opportunity available to an organization in a given market is defined not simply by absolutes such as value or unit size, but by the organization's ability to exploit that market in order to achieve its stated objectives.

WRAP assesses the potential utilization of the overall corporate resource in the light of real time market conditions and corporate expectations. This relies on interpretation of data and on the ability to place this information in its wider context, both within individual territories and in relation to the global marketplace with its competing risks and opportunities.

The nature and value of information

Information can be defined as knowledge derived from study and experience, or gathered by communication, intelligence or news. Information is rarely comprehensive or perfect (ask any government intelligence agency) but is essential in spotting opportunities and, perhaps more critically, reducing or managing risk. It is tempting to claim that more and higher quality information necessarily leads to greater risk reduction, but this claim would have to be modified substantially by the evident reality that poor or prejudiced analysis of information can often lead to misleading or simply wrong conclusions. A significant element of informed and rational judgment is required in balancing the various pieces of information to help eliminate unhelpful prejudices and to link probability into the analytical requirement.

It was Donald Rumsfeld, US Secretary of State for Defense, in referring to his country's difficulties in Iraq, who came up with the often-used quote, 'as we know, there are known knowns. There are things we know we know. We also know there are known unknowns. That is to say, there are some things we do not know. But there are also unknown unknowns, the ones we don't know we don't know.'.

Figure 6.1   Nine Types of Information

1. Information that is true – precision is a rare commodity, but for strategic purposes something close will be adequate
2. Information that corroborates or supports other information
3. Information that is incomprehensible – provided in a form that is confusing
4. Information that is wrong
5. Information that is a lie – likely to be deliberately wrong or misleading
6. Information based on assumption
7. Information based on belief – political, racial, geographic, religious or something else
8. Information that lacks credibility – may be right or wrong, but seems significantly anomalous to other information, comes from a source that is distrusted, or is in some other way viewed with scepticism
9. Information that is irrelevant

The credibility of this statement is perhaps debatable. The objective veracity of most information is open to some degree of scepticism, small or large, and it is our contextual knowledge and judgment that leads us to a belief that a given piece of information is more likely to be closer to true than not. Government intelligence organizations worldwide try (hopefully) to find corroboration for each piece of evidence, and information gains credibility through supporting information from several alternative sources. The WRAP process is deliberately designed to multi-source and compare information within its operational context, so that the risks inherent in interpreting information are substantially reduced.

It is of course possible to develop a purely abstract strategy that can subsequently be superimposed onto the organization regardless of external or internal circumstances. In a related approach a branch of the cognitive school of strategic development argues that the environment essentially exists as it is perceived in the mind of the strategist, who then proceeds to create a model based on this cognitive awareness.[1] While paying due respect to the necessity for and inevitability of individual judgment and interpretation in the strategy process, such an approach can expose an organization to potentially serious difficulties arising from an inability to identify, understand, or respond adequately to autonomous changes in the marketplace. This challenge is particularly acute in international strategy development: foreign markets do operate according to their own rules and perspectives which may be wholly unfamiliar to the strategist, and in order to respond to these successfully it is necessary to engage with them directly rather than relying on a 'model' which may be a more accurate reflection of the strategist's preconceptions than of the market itself. Without a more objective market awareness, it also becomes extremely hard to assess whether the organization's resources are in fact deployed to good effect.

The value of information in strategy development lies ultimately in its ability to situate the strategy in a larger context to which it is responsive, and against which it can be assessed. Information alerts the organization to what is possible, what is desirable, and what is likely to be dangerous or counterproductive.

Information works to limit risk, particularly in global markets, by outlining and amplifying the conditions under which the organization will be required to operate. Since the conditions on the ground will affect the performance of the business in any case, it is prudent to know at the very least what they are and how they function. Information also works to identify constraints on doing business in particular markets, allowing poor investment prospects to be spotted and eliminated at an early stage before they become a long term drain on resources.

More positively, information can help to identify potential for expanding or enhancing business prospects in new or existing markets, and to prioritize markets by permitting comparisons and evaluations that direct the organization's efforts. It also becomes possible to assess corporate performance through measuring market potential and determining whether and where there is scope for improvement. Information provides a focus for corporate investment decisions through permitting a more complete understanding of what is achievable, and at what price. It also enables the organization to utilize its capabilities effectively by providing an indication of how these might be deployed to maximum effect.

Perhaps most importantly, information brings realism to the whole process of strategic development by grounding corporate objectives in actuality, thereby making them truly meaningful as an indication of the organization's direction and mitigating the risk of unrealistic and consequently unachievable objectives acting as a drag on performance and resources, while allowing genuinely useful and practical criteria to be applied to the process of international market development, and thus maintaining continuity of purpose in dynamic markets.

And what does a lack of information provide? It is a gateway to risky opportunism, through which money chases passing opportunities in the hope that something will pan out successfully. It begins to look a great deal like gambling.

Rationale behind information development

Thoughts on the timing and resources to be applied to information development should be focused in the first instance not on the absolute cost of the process, but on understanding how the demand for information affects the overall complexity of strategy development. Information development is not an end in itself, but a tool used to inform and guide the strategy program. The eminently pragmatic function of information development indicates that it must be controlled through its responsiveness to the requirements of the strategy program.

For example, if it is necessary to determine a global strategy for an organization with an existing presence in most national markets, it would seem at first glance that truly practical information development is out of the question. A comprehensive research program in anything up to 300 countries would take years, cost a great deal of money, and provide little actionable feedback in a situation in which decisions must be made and implemented within a relatively tight time frame.

Perhaps more important, the level of detail expected from the development process has direct relevance for the viability of the strategy program. Drawing up very detailed criteria requires commitment to a more complex information development process, with a concomitant risk of becoming bogged down in minutiae, while vague or ill-defined criteria reduce the likelihood that such research can provide any meaningful direction. As a significant input into a strategy program, information derived through research also requires to be analyzed and assessed, in itself a task that becomes exponentially more difficult as information volumes grow.

These provisos serve to indicate that information development needs to be tightly focused in order to function as something more than an extended exercise in fact chasing and data processing. This focus is twofold. It is first of all dependent on the nature of the information that is determined to be most necessary to facilitating strategy development. Secondly, it concentrates on securing and refining the accuracy of this information through ensuring its consistency and comparability.

The information development process

The basic method through which information is developed in a business context is, of course, market or business research in all its various manifestations. A detailed review of research methodology is outside the scope of this book, but an outline of its essential aspects will clarify the way it can be applied to information development for strategic purposes. This will be followed by a more detailed examination of the implications of an international context for information development processes.

In market research terms secondary research refers to the review of existing data and information on specific markets or industries with a view to gleaning information relevant to a given topic of interest. This has the obvious advantage of avoiding the reinvention of the wheel by making use of someone else's hard-won analysis. More subtly, it also acts as a method of orientation in an unfamiliar landscape, suggesting potential directions and opportunities that can be more thoroughly examined through primary research.

Primary research is the process of collecting data and information directly from individuals involved in the relevant market. These may include existing or potential customers, or individuals and organizations active in important aspects of the market such as trade associations, regulatory agencies, government offices, and other public or commercial institutions. Primary market research is usually bespoke research tailored to directly address the specific issues and concerns of a single body, but it also encompasses multi-client studies or omnibus surveys in which the cost of research is shared between participants. In both types of research there is a distinction to be made between quantitative research, which seeks to establish reliable statistical data relating to a market or its component parts, and qualitative research, which is more broadly concerned with understanding the mechanisms by which markets operate and end-user decisions are made. Important differences emerge when comparing research processes for consumer and industrial markets. Consumer research by its nature usually deals with a potentially large number of end-users, and so makes greater use of large scale surveys in which sample size and definition is of key importance in developing statistically respectable survey data. It is also more common to find published market reports covering a range of consumer segments in both industrialized and developing countries.

Industrial markets, which cover products and services sold to business or government, may pose particular difficulties for the researcher. Many industrial products and services fall into niche segments with a comparatively small number of end users, and their willingness to participate in any type of research may be severely constrained by concerns about commercial confidentiality. Specific data on industrial market segments may also be difficult or impossible to find in any readily accessible form simply because it is not of widespread enough interest to merit collection. In such a segment, the issue is effectively less one of absolute statistical accuracy and more a question of becoming able to understand the operation of the market in a qualitative sense through a variety of sources.

Quantitative and qualitative market data can be usefully expanded upon through a country visit to prioritized markets before strategy development takes place. The purpose of a personal visit to a given territory is manifold. It provides an opportunity to confirm, or refute and amend, the market information already assembled, and it offers a means of enhancing qualitative awareness of the market and the manner in which it operates. It offers the manager the opportunity to obtain feedback on market data from participants themselves. The visit also offers a chance to make new and relevant contacts in the market with potential partners, distributors, or customers, which can be further developed as appropriate. In order for a country visit to be of significant use, it is essential to be armed with a significant range of current data and information before making such a trip.

Market research has a vital and well-established role in market development at all levels, but its specific application to information development within a strategy program differs significantly from its traditional role of providing in-depth analysis of the highest possible accuracy. In the context of global strategy, the aim of any type of information development is the establishment of the market priorities that will form the focus of the strategic program.

WRAP requires sufficient information to allow comparison of markets; if information is not readily available, or prohibitively expensive to purchase or research, there must be a means of estimating relevant data. Such a process of estimation may not provide an absolutely accurate indication of market size and composition, but this is not what is required. What is necessary is a means of prioritizing markets in terms of the opportunity offered, encompassing the totality of market conditions. Prioritization is a process of establishing relative importance in order to deliver the vital strategic focus.

The market model

Having defined the objectives, parameters and criteria within which the strategic development program will initially take place, it is possible to begin defining the market model and developing concrete information within it. The market model is intended to provide a snapshot of a territory or region in information terms in order to facilitate comparisons between territories and to provide a guide to the market conditions that the organization can expect to encounter in various territories. This model makes use of both quantitative and qualitative data in building a picture of both the current state of a market and the manner in which it operates, which allows insight into the ways in which a market might change over time.

The model itself is made up of the criteria selected by the organization, supplemented by key comparators and contextual data. Corporate criteria will form the focus of the market model. These criteria should, as previously described, be reasonably specific and should in themselves suggest the type of data now required. If further guidance is necessary, the organization's domestic market can in certain respects act as a comparator on a global scale.

Key comparators refer to quantitative information that will be of use in making overall comparisons between countries and their respective markets, and which are not addressed directly by the corporate criteria. Key comparators are additionally vital in situations in which it is necessary to extrapolate missing data, as they provide a platform for making data estimates based on the performance of markets and their characteristics in comparable territories. These may include GDP, economic growth rates, population size, or other features of the territory.

Key comparators also provide a background against which data relating to corporate criteria can be interpreted. Contextual data, as the name suggests, is usually made up of qualitative factors that provide essential market context. Alongside key comparators, contextual data are used to amplify awareness of the market and assist the organization in taking into account factors that may have a major influence on the interpretation of criteria. Contextual data also reveals potential sources of risk operating within the territory which may not be directly connected to the product market itself, but which may have a critical influence over the organization's operations in the territory.

In the event that the chosen parameters have not already defined a geographical center of interest, it is initially useful to consider the world on a regional basis, defined by geographic proximity as well as by the larger political and economic associations in which territories are involved. These associations may well be a key influence on market operation within and across a range of territories, and they may also have implications for market extension at some point in the future. Depending on strategic direction, there may be an evident logistical benefit in focusing on a region for the purposes of distribution or local manufacture.

Information development is also handled more easily by regionalizing the global marketplace. Significant information on territories and markets is often available from institutions including regional development banks and supranational organizations, such as the directorates of the European Union and relevant parts of the United Nations Organization. Individuals working within national markets may additionally have experience in locating and utilizing information from neighboring territories, and may be able to provide useful guidance in this respect. Most importantly, regional comparisons will be necessary for estimating data that is otherwise unavailable, a process which will be covered in more detail below.

Although these wider associations may enhance the complexity of the market, they do not define its totality. It is important at this stage not to be misled by declarations that the global market is now a homogeneous entity. In the first instance, much detailed information development will be done primarily on a country-by-country basis as this is, in practice, the principle way in which statistical data and other information is provided both by public sector bodies and private organizations. More critically, country-specific contexts and practices also determine the general shape of the legal, regulatory, and cultural frameworks within which the organization will need to work in both a marketing and an operational sense. For the purposes of international strategy development, the nation state is alive and well.

Building the market model

After definition and application of the parameters previously outlined, it is possible to begin building the market model. As discussed in Chapter 5, parameters operate to limit the scope of enquiry either on a geographical basis, or by eliminating territories displaying particular characteristics that have been identified as undesirable or which are likely in some way to restrict market opportunity. In the case of technological parameters some rudimentary research may be required to uncover which territories fall outside the scope of the defined parameters, but this should be done rapidly, without going into detail at this point. For example, a company that develops software for use within the legal system pertaining to England and Wales may set a single parameter: requiring target markets to possess a legal system based on that of England, as its software could be most readily adapted for such markets. At this early stage it is necessary only to arrive at the most basic definition of which may territories meet this requirement and which do not, without delving further into territorial or market data.

Figure 6.2   The Saga of the Broken Window

A small firm that manufactured translucent plastic safety sheets for emergency application to broken windows decided to search for a distributor in South Africa. The managing director reasoned that this territory had many vandals and thus many broken windows, particularly in what were formerly the African townships. He failed to find a distributor largely because such windows generally had no glass to be broken in the first place. His next idea was to identify areas of heavy vandalism that actually did have glass windows, and settled accordingly on northern Italy on the assumption that it was a heavily industrialized area that was likely to be subject to vandalism. At this point his advisor suggested that the real targets for his products were more likely to be found in locations in which individuals or institutions felt compelled to address the issue of broken windows, rather than identified through a perceived propensity to vandalism.

The firm re-orientated its parameters accordingly and Germany became its first export market. Italy was also reinstated as a target, but this time for the right reasons.

Application of parameters leaves a core of territories, either worldwide or within a specific region, for each of which a comprehensive market model will be developed. The market model is at the heart of the information development process, and relies on a balance of quantitative and qualitative data that will permit comparisons between territories, and ultimately determine prioritization of markets. The definition of the data and information to be collected is critical to the coherence and usefulness of the model and must be considered with care. It is during this model building stage that two basic problems are likely to arise. First of all, how can we know precisely what information is really necessary for a program of market prioritization that will deliver according to corporate objectives? And furthermore, how can its accuracy be assured, particularly in situations in which the analyst has so little inherent knowledge of the territory that it seems virtually impossible to assess the data?

Although it is not constructive to attempt to define an information outline that will be valid for every organization in all situations, it is possible and useful to consider what issues this information is intended to address. First of all, information must allow comparisons to be made between territories based on the identified corporate criteria. Information must also permit a wider comprehension of fundamental characteristics that ultimately have an effect on the immediate market within a territory. Finally, the information obtained should allow the strategic analyst to develop an awareness of the risks inherent in each territory.

Ensuring the accuracy and validity of any information is critical to information development. How is it possible to know whether information presents a true picture of the market, or is simply noise? Initially, the problem is most effectively overcome by making use of reliable sources who themselves have a stake in understanding the real situation in given territory. These may include government statistical offices, non-governmental organizations, or national or regional trade and industry associations.

Cross-referencing data and information across published or bespoke sources and balancing it against the experience of individuals working in the market is a practical means of gaining a more reasoned perspective of the information at the organization's disposal. It is unlikely that all quantitative data obtained will tally exactly, but this is in any case unnecessary; the strategist is seeking reasonable correlation of orders of magnitude in the comparison of data. Knowing whether a market is worth exactly $300 million or $800 million is less important than having confidence that a market is most probably worth, in the current year, between $400 and $600 million, and likely to be growing at a rate of 7–10 per cent. Similarly, qualitative information does not always lend itself to absolute precision, nor can it provide guarantees of performance within a territory. Nonetheless it is useful to know that Territory A boasts a legal system with a record of protecting the IP rights of both domestic and foreign organizations, while Territory B appears to have laws on the books that may not be reliably invoked in practice.

As a precautionary measure the risk of deliberate misinformation must be taken into account, but in practice a reasonable amount of vigilance minimizes this problem. It's highly unlikely that everyone in a given market would be misleading another participant with the same false trails of information. However, it is entirely possible that critical information can be misinterpreted or even ignored because its significance is obscured by cultural differences, and on this theme we refer the reader back to Chapters 3 and 4 for a review of this critical topic. It is at this point that personal judgment and market information need to be utilized as interactive components of the strategy development process: judgment needs to be informed by real-world data, and information must be interpreted in a manner consistent with the priorities of the market. 'Common sense' is not in practice an adequate description of the cognitive processes required. In an alternative cultural context, common sense may look uncommonly strange.

India, for example, exemplifies a number of such issues that have been known to defeat the common sense of Western managers. Because unskilled or semi-skilled labor is very cheap, and unemployment attracts no benefits through any welfare system, it is common practice in this territory for people to try to ensure that there is sufficient income for those who are employed to support the survival of an entire family. For example, everyone of working age may be given some small tasks to do in return for some pay. This can lead to many situations simply not understood by western or international businesses, in which the efficiency of a mechanized process can be completely undermined by the need to employ numbers of bodies in order to avoid starvation. There are, of course, anomalies even in this apparently simple approach. One of these is in the maintenance of machinery and equipment, where spares are often manufactured (rather than purchased) in a workshop round the corner if this is technically possible. Otherwise, machines that have broken down can be abandoned and ignored as in many cases no budget has been allowed for the purchase of maintenance from overseas. It might be assumed that in these circumstances there would be sufficient people, as well as sufficient motivation to avoid literal starvation, that would ensure the development of a huge force of repair and maintenance staff, but outside the main industrial centers there is often no facility for retraining or reorientating a largely agrarian population to undertake these tasks. This represents a principal example of the type of contextual information that is critical to the prioritization process. In a straightforward analysis India may appear as a large and growing market for manufacturing equipment, but this may be offset by on-the-spot cultural or working practices than could cast a different light on market prioritization.

Key comparators and contextual information

As previously described key comparators and contextual information are general data sets used as a supplement to defined corporate criteria. Their importance lies in their ability to inform the market model by providing a background against which criteria can be interpreted and analyzed more thoroughly. They also provide a basis on which crucial data can, if necessary, be extrapolated and fed into the market model.

Key comparators

In terms of defining key comparators, the strategist is seeking hard data that will situate the corporate criteria within a wider national framework. Comparators comprise general statistical data relating to a territory that is both readily available and commonly accepted as an accurate depiction of the status of the territory. Topics amenable to this type of quantification include those for which definite statistical data can be identified or generated, such as GDP size and growth, market size, demographic statistics and trends, domestic production levels, and similar sets of data.

As an example, it is evident from the information supplied in Figure 6.3 that of the five countries reviewed, France has the wealthiest inhabitants and Indonesia the poorest.

Figure 6.3   Example of Quantitative Comparators

Country	GDP 2002 (current prices, US$ billions)	GDP growth (forecast) (%)	GDP per capita (US$)
France	1,431.3	1.2	23,855
Italy	1,184.3	0.4	20,419
Malaysia	95.2	4.2	3,917
Indonesia	172.9	3.7	82
India	447.0	7.1	447

Sources: World Bank, OECD

By way of analysis, however, it may be considered useful to apply Pareto's Law to the latter 3 territories. That is, we assume 20 per cent of the population accounts for 80 per cent of the wealth; in that case GDP per capita for the wealthier elements of society begins to look more like this:

Malaysia	US$15,232
Indonesia	US$2,766
India	US$7,102

On this basis, Malaysia can now be perceived as containing a small population wealthier than some European territories such as Spain and Portugal, while the calculations for the other two territories suggest that they might also contain significant numbers of potential consumers. Consider this: 20 per cent of India's population is 200 million people, almost three times larger than Germany, while 20 per cent of Indonesia's population is around 20 million people. This amounts to a significant potential consumer market in territories in which the bulk of the population is rightly assumed to be very poor indeed.

As an alternative, recalculating these figures at purchasing power parity (PPP) would indicate that the three poorer countries have greater purchasing power than the above figures suggest. PPP, however, tells an in-country story that would be useful if a foreign firm were setting up a manufacturing plant or office in the territory but counts for little for firms seeking to sell goods or services whose manufacturing costs are attributed elsewhere. Similarly, if we consider potential consumer markets in Western Europe as a further example, total population may give us a guide to priorities in the region.

As an initial comparator for a consumer sector, these figures help to set market potential in context. From the data in Figure 6.4 it can easily be seen that Germany has the largest potential consumer market, and that the top five countries together dominate western Europe. Of course, the great majority of markets will require significant segmentation before the strategist arrives at a proper understanding of actual market potential. If such segmentation is readily identifiable through available sources so much the better, but in practice it is likely to require a degree of extrapolation, as discussed below. In this case general population data will be necessary as a basis of information from which estimates can be derived.

Contextual information

Contextual information refers to qualitative data that is utilized to provide further background information on a territory in order to

Figure 6.4   Some Populations in Western Europe

Country	Population (millions)
Germany	82
Italy	60
UK	59
France	58
Spain	42
Netherlands	15
Belgium	10
Greece	10
Portugal	9
Austria	8
Sweden	8
Switzerland	6
Finland	5
Denmark	4
Norway	4
Ireland	4

Source: national statistics

round out the market model. This type of information is particularly important is assessing risks and opportunities in a given territory that may not become apparent through the analysis of statistical data alone, and as such its significance is more diffuse and cannot generally be profitably expressed in numerical terms. Such information is likely to encompass such issues as the nature and efficacy of the legal system, political organization and stability, potential threats to personal or commercial security, or the relative sophistication of the domestic customer base or existing competitors in the territory.

Contextual factors, like key comparators, are intended to be brought into play after the key criteria have been matched as a means of further evaluating the territory. The criteria used for developing a market model are supplemented by these contextual and comparative items of national information, so that the results reflect on-the-ground reality and comparisons of criteria can be cross-referenced by means of both standard and qualitative data.

Figure 6.5 provides an example of some simple rankings that might be employed over a small range of qualitative factors and is predicated on assumed levels of risk as follows:

1 = Low risk
2 = Moderate risk
3 = High risk

Figure 6.5 Ranking Contextual Factors Across Territories

Country / Factor	Country 1	Country 2	Country 3	Country 4
Political system	Absolute monarchy Ranking: 2	Democracy Ranking: 1	Democracy Ranking: 1	Socialist Ranking: 2
Legal system	Religious law Ranking: 3	Established commercial law Ranking: 1	Established commercials law Ranking: 1	Limited commercial law Ranking: 2
Business orientation	Open economy Ranking: 1	Capitalist Ranking: 1	Open economy Ranking: 1	Limited open economy Ranking: 2
Personal security	Low crime/ high risk of terrorism Ranking: 3	High crime/ low risk of terrorism Ranking: 2	Low crime/ war outside cities Ranking: 2	Low crime/ no risk of terrorism Ranking: 1
TOTAL	9	5	5	7

Ranking contextual factors necessarily requires some knowledge of the territory to be brought to bear on the subject. It also requires the strategist to make a judgment about the ability of the organization to operate successfully within the framework that obtains within the territory.

In this example, the lower the total score, then less risk is involved, but it should be stressed that each factor carries its own weight according to the requirements and situation of each company. A firm based in a Muslim territory, for example, might have an entirely different point of view regarding the factors relating to 'country 1', while someone from Mongolia might perceive a socialist territory as far less risky than a highly competitive capitalist country.

It may also be argued that, under certain conditions, issues of risk and opportunity become immaterial. This is often true of resource extraction companies such as mining concerns or oil companies, as well as their associated suppliers. The geographic location of mines and oilfields dictates that such organizations may well be constrained to operate in environments replete with risks of varying types and degrees. However, this simply suggests that such organizations, in order to continue in business at all, require to optimize their operations in order to manage such risk and ensure an appropriate level of return.

Data extrapolation

During the information development process it may become obvious that reliable quantitative information will in fact be hard to come by in certain territories in which official statistics are less comprehensive, or where the relevant market segment does not attract the attention of either official statisticians or firms producing commercial research reports. In some countries, or in market segments that are highly sensitive for technical or security reasons, there may also be a general reluctance amongst individuals involved in the market to speak frankly about its composition and prospects, and consequently little assistance or guidance can be expected from them.

Ideally, the answer to this problem would be a full scale bespoke research project that attempts to nail down every aspect of the market, but as already noted this approach is prohibitively expensive across a range of territories as well as exceedingly time-consuming in the context of a strategy program. It is therefore necessary, if any informed assessment of the market is to be made, to build extrapolated data using appropriate comparisons and estimates based on available information.

As the great but long deceased Aristotle observed in the Nichomachean Ethics, 'it is the mark of an educated mind to rest satisfied with the degree of precision that the subject admits, and not to seek exactness when only approximation is possible.' This is extremely valuable advice for anyone tasked with estimating data for use in practical decision-making. Nevertheless, estimating data for the purposes of setting strategic priorities does require that the approximations are sufficiently realistic to allow this task to be effectively performed.

This in turn requires that extrapolations are founded on the most reliable data available. In most territories this is likely to be key comparators such as essential economic and demographic information. Experience in the application of the WRAP process has shown that two general rules should be applied:

1. Estimates should best be made with data that is available in countries with similar or related economic, business, culture and wealth factors, normally to be found in the same region. This is particularly valuable in situations in which the data sought is more readily accessible in some territories than in others. Such an approach allows the strategist to examine relevant sets of data from each

territory in an effort to understand relationships within it and to utilize these in extrapolating data for countries in which statistics are not available. This also facilitates comparisons between territories as an aid to the prioritization process.

2. The range of data pertaining to each missing factor to be estimated can be narrowed by reference to population size.

For example, it is possible to estimate the probable size of the market for police cars in Saudi Arabia if the market size is known in UAE and Kuwait, as all three territories are reasonably similar in economic structure, culture and relative wealth, and the key difference in this instance is the size of the population. As an alternative, however, if the market size is unknown in all three territories, then it will be necessary first to calculate the size of each police force and then work out a ratio for numbers of police to each car. These methods, however complex they may sound, still provide a sufficiency of information much more quickly and cheaply than conventional market research, which in this situation would be very difficult or impossible to carry out in any case.

Figure 6.6   International Police

A large UK-based firm manufactured uniforms for police forces in a number of countries around the world and had developed a protective jacket that it hoped to add to its product portfolio. Although most developed countries hold at least some publicly available information on police forces and their equipment levels, Africa proved to be a different story. In many countries in the region the police uniform itself is not regularly issued, and its acquisition may depend on the demise or retirement of other members of the police force. Furthermore, although sales volumes shipped to the firm's customers in Africa were known, it was not known what proportion of the relevant police force was properly equipped with the uniforms, nor was there any awareness of the procurement cycles for new uniform acquisitions. Determining a potential market size for the new jacket was a virtual impossibility in the region other than using knowledge of the area, judgment on probabilities and estimates based on data from a few of the more forthcoming territories.

The issue was quite acute as Africa represented a significant proportion of the firm's business, but it was determined that while the protective jacket seemed to be a popular concept in the minds of the African purchasing authorities, there was likely to be insufficient actual demand as the level of funds available for what would be regarded as a semi-luxury security item would not comprise a sufficient market size.

Having completed the information development program, it is possible to assess the territories and begin the process of global market prioritization. The evaluation of commercial opportunity and risk in a given territory is at this stage tied back to the corporate objectives already outlined. It is at this point that crucial issues of judgment are brought into play with regard to both the genuine market opportunities available, as well as the ultimate validity of the corporate objectives themselves.

Note

1 Henry Mintzberg, Bruce Ahlstrand, and Joseph Lampel, *Strategy Safari*. London: Pearson Education, 1998

7
Analysis and Strategic Prioritization

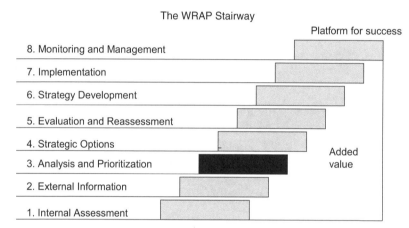

The WRAP Stairway

Platform for success

8. Monitoring and Management

7. Implementation

6. Strategy Development

5. Evaluation and Reassessment

4. Strategic Options

Added value

3. Analysis and Prioritization

2. External Information

1. Internal Assessment

This chapter discusses ways in which information can be analyzed and priorities determined.

All the effort in the WRAP process to this point has been focused on creating sound foundations for building a successful strategy for international business development through the assessment of internal and external circumstances influencing the organization's operation and prospects in non-domestic markets. The next step in the staircase is utilizing this information to re-establish focus through prioritizing markets and interests that best match the parameters and criteria selected. It is worth emphasizing that the key reasons for climbing this staircase are twofold:–

- The information serves to limit risk and identify real opportunity
- The strategies to be developed are based on assessment of the company's ambitions, capabilities, resources and strengths

Thus far, prioritization has operated through two steps of the WRAP process. Step 1 encompassed the assessment of the organization's internal capabilities, and Step 2 has focused on the development of necessary external information. This initially involved the definition of parameters and criteria as a means of ranking territories against key market characteristics and creating the first part of the market model. This market model, which is key to the prioritization process, is composed of criteria plus key comparators and contextual data. This market model is intended to delineate a picture of the market in information terms, as a means of providing a guide to what the strategist might expect to find in that market.

The creation of a market model, or of alternative regional models, allows comparisons to be made of the parts of markets that are most relevant to the organization and the products or services it provides. Obviously, there is little point in comparing population sizes around the world if an organization is focusing on offshore oil and gas extraction, as it would be far more important to identify known oil and gas fields as well as new discoveries and areas showing geological promise. Equally, population size is highly relevant to consumer industries, preferably segmented by disposable income, age or other factors of significance to the manufacturer or supplier.

These steps are described in Figure 7.1, bringing together the elements of the WRAP process already completed to indicate the way in which they feed into the prioritization process. This is the beginning of ensuring that strategies can be properly focused, based on realistic information that is responsive to strategic objectives.

Figure 7.1   Elements in the Prioritization Process

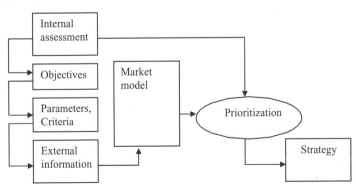

The specific form of the market model may vary, but the critical issue is that the information that relates to the criteria needs to be displayed in a style amenable to cross-comparison. Using spreadsheets or similar arrangements organized by region, country and criteria factors is generally a very effective means of keeping a wide range of information in a meaningful yet readily accessible format. The system of ranking quali-

Figure 7.2 Healthcare in Colombia

Colombia is a very beautiful country in South America that has coasts and beaches on both the Pacific Ocean and the Caribbean Sea. Unfortunately the CIA World Factbook tells us that, 'a 40 year insurgent campaign to overthrow the Colombian government escalated during the 1990s, undergirded in part by funds from the drug trade. Although the violence is deadly and large swathes of the countryside are under guerrilla influence, the movement lacks the military strength or popular support necessary to overthrow the government. An anti-insurgent army of paramilitaries has grown to several thousand strong in recent years, challenging the insurgents for control of territory and illicit industries such as the drug trade. While Bogota steps up efforts to reassert government authority throughout the country, neighboring countries worry about the violence spilling over its borders.'

Another quote from the same source is, 'Colombia's economy suffers from weak domestic and foreign demand, austere government budgets and serious internal armed conflict.' And into this poor country stepped a European healthcare trade association bent on targeting Colombia as a priority business prospect for its members. So how did this arise?

The trade association operated a program that involved searching for alternative export territories that would be likely to offer significant growth markets for its members' goods and services. The principle criterion used to identify suitable territories was the existence of increases in national healthcare budgets over the domestic rate of inflation. Theoretically, this would indicate a growing market for healthcare products in the territory. On this basis it was calculated that Colombia ranked quite high on its list of priority markets.

In this instance, poor criteria selection was combined with an inadequate appreciation of critical contextual and comparative information. Examining increases in national healthcare budgets is a useful indicator of market size only in territories with a large state sector, as commonly found in Europe and certain other countries such as Canada; it is entirely unhelpful in territories in which state healthcare provision is either limited or nonexistent. Furthermore, a bare statistic viewed without context can turn out to be a very problematic piece of data. The putative budget increase provided no information about the shape or operation of the Columbian healthcare system, or even whether the private healthcare sector was larger than the government-funded sector. Perhaps more importantly, it offered no indication of any security issues relevant to the territory. The utilization of poorly-selected criteria may indeed lead to ill-advised enthusiasm for inappropriate markets that turn out to be not only unprofitable but, as in this case, potentially dangerous.

Needless to say, the members showed substantially less enthusiasm for investing valuable resources in this market, quickly identifying the multiple risks inherent in the territory – low demand, relatively poor population, poor distribution outside Bogota, significant personal danger, to mention just a few difficulties – and moving their interest up the priority ladder to more stable territories.

tative data, as discussed in Chapter 6, permits the strategist to keep this data easily at hand; in addition, and extended spreadsheet format provides a means for those elements of qualitative information that cannot be easily ranked to be held ready to come into play when required.

Recognizing the corporate subtext

The market model itself, although it offers an excellent tool for deliberate analysis and prioritization, only takes account of the requirements of the stated objectives, parameters and criteria. Organizations also have subtexts that can entirely override the results of the formal analysis if they are not identified at an early stage and taken into consideration. By 'subtext' we refer to an unspoken assumption, or set of assumptions, that may have a material influence on the way the organization reacts to market conditions, or the way it approaches opportunities identified in either domestic or global markets. Such corporate assumptions often remain unarticulated because organizational hierarchies may be uncomfortable with challenges to them that suggest a desire for change, or because these assumptions underpin existing centers of authority within the organization.

For example, company politics may play a major role in creating an unacknowledged subtext that needs to be taken into account during the strategy development process. Although internal organizational politics can manifest themselves in myriad ways, it is often the case that latent resistance to the process may reside in existing organizational power bases, where the individuals involved may be concerned about the potential loss of corporate clout or influence attendant upon strategic change. This problem can be acute in organizations with a strong domestic base, or with a developed global structure already in place. In such a case, members of some part of the existing organizational structure may perceive a shift in resources towards new or alternate strategic targets to be a threat either to their own resource levels, or their corporate position. Additional internal political stresses can be generated when there is a question of cross-cultural management or working practices being introduced into the organization, which may not be uniformly welcomed by all employees.

Equally pervasive and significant are the organic sources of strategic stress within the organization. For example, the board of a publicly quoted company generally has a responsibility to provide investment value for its shareholders, and it is one of the roles of a CEO to consider that investment value in leading corporate activities. In practice, organizations in different countries take different views of the way that value is translated into shareholder fortune. Stock market led economies, such as the United States and the UK, tend to look to shareholder dividends and stock trading profits within a relatively short time frame. Conversely, countries where family shareholdings are in many cases the largest element in corporate control, such as Japan, Germany and Italy, tend to take a longer term approach that reflects the family need to sustain corporate value over generations. The strengths and demerits of each aspect of this argument have been discussed many times over in countless articles and publications; from a strategy development perspective the importance of being aware of these subtexts and taking them into account during the prioritization process is critical in ensuring that strategies, once developed, can be fully implemented without sudden disruption from an unexpected source of conflict.

The effect of this particular argument can be demonstrated in a tale of three companies in the same industry sector, all operating in a niche market providing services to healthcare. The first company is American and made a decision to focus entirely on increasing profitability in its North American operations, thus avoiding further major capital expenditure and the risk entailed in expanding overseas. Its shareholders like it and it provides substantial shareholder value.

The second company is European and for many years was reluctant to invest beyond its domestic frontiers as pricing and returns there were higher than could be found elsewhere. Eventually, having built up its cash reserves to a point where the relatively low interest rates available threatened to upset its accustomed profitability levels, it expanded by acquiring one of its European competitors which it estimated could be brought to a similar level of profitability. The third company was born in America and already had substantial European operations before it was acquired by another European firm, this time privately owned. The strategy employed was one of developing world dominance through investment in plant and equipment, and after a few lean years the company effectively achieved its objective. It is now so much larger than its key competitors that while it can be challenged on a local basis it would take many years for another organization to develop a global challenge. Readers may perceive this situation differently, but as we see it Company 3 is now providing its shareholders with a growing return on investment as well as improving business value; Company 2 is moving to a position where its profitability is unlikely to be as high as a few years ago, but its prospects for stability and growth are much improved; and Company 1 has demonstrated the shareholder benefits of focusing on North America but remains vulnerable to competition, particularly from foreign competitors seeking a foothold in the large and stable North American market.

Nor is this the only subtext that can make itself apparent as strategy development proceeds. Some of the better-known alternative agendas include:–

- *Financial resources.* The organization may be motivated by the need to conserve capital, or the need to conserve revenue expenditure.
- *Status.* Where does a company or brand of a given status and reputation need to be to demonstrate to its competitors and customers its global presence? Serious global pretensions require activity to back them up, and this means identifying key global markets and developing presence there despite any organizational hesitation or fear.
- *Operational issues.* The organization may have a cast-iron belief that products must be manufactured in the domestic market and exported because there is domestic spare capacity, or because there is an organizational reluctance to shift any manufacturing capacity away from the home territory.

These issues need to be borne in mind and ultimately addressed as the strategy develops. For example, a strategy in course of development might need to be 'tweaked' to take account of the different perceptions of an American as compared to a German firm. For the American company, the strategy may require to provide some deliverable returns at an early stage in order to meet the demands of shareholders and management, while a similar strategy for a German company may offer the company medium to longer-term stability of return and a prospect of continuing steady growth.

Of course, the corporate subtext may be identified and accounted for within the organization's internal assessment and strategic objectives. However, the situation often arises that existence of such a subtext does not become plain until the prioritization process is underway: once the strategic direction begins to become clearer, sources of resistance to it will be more readily identifiable. It is not necessarily the case that these subtexts will in all cases be flexible or amenable to change, but it is necessary that they be identified and acknowledged before strategy formulation takes place. Indeed, this is probably one of the strongest arguments for using external help in developing strategies as different subtexts can emanate from various parts of the corporate entity and counteract each other, sometimes to destructive effect.

Gaining focus: the prioritization process

As we have seen thus far, the information development process fleshes out the market model, which describes territories and/or regions in information terms. The market model is then subjected to strategic prioritization: the territories that offer the best fit with the organization's objectives and criteria are now prioritized for strategic development. This provides the organizational focus to ensure that investment is commensurate with expected returns in the market and is not simply bled away through uncoordinated expenditure. Having examined the information development process in abstract terms, we will now look at its practical application within the framework of market prioritization.

In working through the WRAP process parameters and criteria must be identified first, as they initially define the shape of the information development process and make it possible for the strategist to make a judgment about which key comparators and contextual factors will need to be assessed in order to provide an adequate background for successful strategy development. Subsequently, however, the research process itself begins by generating data for key comparators and then for contextual factors, focusing in finally on the criteria. In the WRAP process information development ideally moves from broad and general information to the most specific information, gradually narrowing the scope of enquiry and allowing the strategist to begin the task of prioritizing certain territories over others. This approach also eases the task of developing adequate data for the selected criteria through permitting an early-stage prioritization of territories, excluding those that appear to offer less scope for meeting corporate objectives.

Territories that are excluded at an early stage may ultimately be drawn back in to the rollout of any strategy developed. However, these early exclusions mean that much time and effort can be saved by focusing successive stages of information development on those territories most likely to be of interest, and therefore to become priority targets. As each layer of information is reviewed and compared across territories it will quickly become evident which countries and which markets should be considered as targets, and thus the effort involved in information analysis becomes progressively more focused. There is a shift from concentration on exclusions to concentration on definite inclusions as criteria are matched against country and market conditions, and this search typically becomes more intense as countries that broadly match criteria come under greater scrutiny lower down the criteria list.

Let us return to Smith and Co., our American medical device manufacturer, whose strategic parameters excluded everything outside western Europe. We recall that the organization has selected the following five criteria, ranked in order of importance:–

• Significant home device market
• Appropriate pricing levels
• Market growth potential
• Established distributor network
• Presence of competitive products

The key comparators necessary to place these criteria within a wider territorial framework can be listed as:–

• National populations
• Levels of national wealth, including per capita GDP
• Level of imports for identical or similar products

Relevant contextual factors are in this case mainly known to the company. Smith & Co. have prior experience of a number of European markets through their distributor network, and consequently they have no particular concerns about political, economic, or legal stability in these territories. The company knows that its heart monitoring device is compliant with regulatory requirements in existing markets relating to consumer electrical devices. The threat of random terrorist violence is of concern to the management, primarily in terms of its potential impact on consumer confidence; however, the V-P Business Development believes that this threat is now present in every market, including the US, and that the best means of minimizing its potential effects is through a program of geographic diversification.

Consider the next practical problem. Even excluding EU accession territories, western Europe may be considered to include up to twenty countries, all of which theoretically require a distinctive market model to facilitate informed assessment of priority territories. In order to avoid researching all necessary information in up to twenty countries, it is necessary to provide an initial level of focus by developing information relating to the key comparators; this allows us to exclude countries likely to be of more limited interest and perhaps unable to meet Smith and Co's more specific criteria. The population table at Figure 7.3, reproduced from Chapter 6, makes it evident that the 'big five' of Germany, Italy, UK, France and Spain are likely to provide the largest markets for the product on offer, and therefore it is decided that all other territories will be excluded from further review at this point.

Figure 7.3   Some Population Sizes in Western Europe

Country	Population (millions)
Germany	82
Italy	60
UK	59
France	58
Spain	42
Netherlands	15
Belgium	10
Greece	10
Portugal	9
Austria	8
Sweden	8
Switzerland	6
Finland	5
Denmark	4
Norway	4
Ireland	4

Source: national statistics

It is useful at this stage to discuss in more detail the issue of market size, which has become particularly prevalent in international business circles over the past few years. A range of arguments have been adduced in favor of focusing on small markets at the expense of larger territories. The thinking behind this has hinged primarily on the potentially greater accessibility of smaller markets. These are sometimes perceived to be less competitive, at least in part because they may contain fewer domestic competitors and are therefore likely to be more receptive to imported products. Conversely, large markets are perceived to attract a comparatively large number of foreign competitors, all fighting for a slice of the action. Smaller markets may also offer more options in terms of distribution and partnership opportunities, which may not be available in highly competitive environments where large competitors have already monopolized the most effective channels.

These arguments are not without merit. An organization inexperienced in international business may well find it easier in the first instance to approach a smaller market that shows a high level of imports in a specific segment, rather than trying to compete head-to-head against well-entrenched and experienced domestic companies in a large market. Similarly, organizations with constraints on production levels may actively seek smaller markets as a means of avoiding the dilemmas inherent in undersupplying a large and demanding market. However, the real challenge for the global manager is to understand which approach to the market is most appropriate given the organization's own capabilities, constraints and objectives.

In practice, the suitability of a given market is principally dependent on the return on investment it is possible to draw from the territory. A large market may in fact be more difficult to enter, but once the organization has learned how the market operates and has begun to establish itself in the territory it has a much wider field into which it can extend its business. Smaller markets, by definition, are likely to offer more limited scope in the longer term.

The crux of the issue is that the initial level of investment required to gain market access may not differ significantly between markets, but in a larger market it can be leveraged to much greater effect. Accordingly, the strategist who wishes to champion the approach to a smaller market needs to be very clear that problems of accessibility or supply in large markets will be so difficult or costly to overcome that they are likely to reduce the value of any potential returns to a level that is no longer acceptable to the organization. It is evident that this does not eliminate smaller markets by definition; rather, it forces companies to directly address their reasons for avoiding large territories that would seem to offer more long-term potential. Looking ahead to the discussion of trade barriers in Chapter 8, the simple idea that a market is inherently too 'competitive' or 'hostile' is an inadequate basis on which to avoid large markets that may pose particular challenges to successful entry.

Our experience suggests that, once parameters have been drawn, it is most productive to examine large territories in order to make an initial assessment of them. By working through key comparators and contextual information, large territories can be identified and initially assessed to see whether they conform to the most basic comparators and whether conditions there are consonant with the organization's expectations from the contextual information.

In the example, the next key comparator for consideration is the issue of relative wealth and disposable income. The Smith heart monitor is not a clinical device, but is intended to provide a means of keeping health-conscious consumers in touch with their cardiac condition so that they can alert their own doctor if they suspect a problem is developing. Necessarily, this device will be bought and installed privately. For this reason it is important to having a basic understanding of relative wealth in the territories under consideration.

Figure 7.4 shows GDP per capita for each of the five countries under review. This indicates that the general population in Spain may have less disposable income in hand for this purpose, which might suggest that pricing levels would not be as high as in some of the other territories.

Figure 7.4 Selected GDP Per Capita, 2003

Country	GDP per capita
Germany	US$26,200
Italy	US$25,100
UK	US$25,500
France	US$26,000
Spain	US$21,200

Source: national statistics

These figures can be compared with GDP per capita in the US for the same period, which at US$37,600 is higher than all of these countries and suggests that a larger proportion of the population has an ability to sustain the higher pricing levels required by Smith & Co. Indeed, if pricing levels were the key criteria, this might introduce countries such as Switzerland and Norway to the prioritization process at this point.

Adding the criteria data to this mix of information provides the company with a ranking order for addressing the four territories targeted at this point. It is not unusual, however, that the time frame for potential market development will vary between countries, and thus consideration requires to be given during the development of strategies to the utilization of a rolling approach that focuses on identified opportunity for market entry in each target territory rather than relying entirely on specific rankings.

The matching of criteria is achieved on a comparative basis across territories so that the comparisons can be easily seen and noted. While this may seem ostensibly simplistic, it is remarkable how many firms first target a priority country, and then proceed to search hopefully

Figure 7.5   The Man from the West: A Reprise

Attentive readers will recall our Man from the West, introduced in Chapter 2. He was responsible for the global expansion of his US-based firm engaged in mechanical construction, and who possessed initially a most hazy idea of how to identify truly sound potential markets. Let's look more closely at the way this problem was worked through using the WRAP process. In the first instance, the organization needed to set parameter(s) identifying the scope of the enquiry:

Parameter: Territories possessing US military installations. All others excluded.

Next, the organization needed to identify criteria to be used in assessing the market for their particular service. In this case there was one principle criterion:

Criterion: Installations with a requirement for mechanical construction. In terms of their offering, this would include airfields and naval installations, and exclude simple army bases.

Key comparators need to be identified that would provide a background and framework for the criterion:

Key comparators: Size of US military presence at specific installations.
Number of US military installations in a single territory.

Finally, the contextual information that fleshes out the market model must be articulated:

Contextual information: Physical accessibility of the territory.
Physical security of employees and equipment.

Through developing information of this type, the Man from the West was able to look at a more manageable range of territories suitable for further analysis.

---

within it for opportunities. The WRAP process searches within a region to identify the least risk, most appropriate opportunity for business development with the range of target territories, allowing this strategic approach to determine the nature and pace of market development. Government activity in this area of economic development, such as sponsored trade missions, also tends to favor the former approach, largely because government foreign representation in the form of embassies and trade bodies is usually organized on an individual country basis and opportunities are identified and promoted accordingly. It is incumbent on companies to carefully utilize this information and to themselves select the territories to be targeted, based on their own strategic requirements.

Smith and Co's criteria matches can now be addressed. Figure 7.6 describes an appropriate layout for this information that allows for cross-country comparison without pre-defining either opportunity or strategy.

Figure 7.6   Criteria Matches
(Sample table: left intentionally blank)

Country/criteria	Germany	Italy	France	UK
Market size Market pricing Market growth Distributor network Competitor presence				

Within this example the information entered, depending on the information available, might be expressed as:–

Market size:	value or volume, range of value or volume, large/medium/small
Market pricing:	retail/wholesale price or price range, high/medium/low
Market growth:	annual percentage growth, growing/stable/decline
Distributor network:	existence or number of distributors
Competitor presence:	known competitors by name or number, market share, nature of presence (for example sales office/distributor)

There is a further component that has rated little mention so far, and that is the strength of domestic suppliers compared with imported products. This information can provide an invaluable guide to strategy development as it helps to identify the acceptability of imported products. A current high level of imports is more likely to indicate a greater potential business opportunity for a new import; a low level of imports suggests preference for domestic supply, for whatever reason, which is likely to increase the effort required to open the market.

In a more complex development these assessments might cover up to forty or fifty countries and perhaps a dozen criteria but should be organized in regions, across regions or by area to allow for reasonable quantitative estimates to be calculated where required. Sometimes it is appropriate to utilize the information in different comparisons, to gain alternative perceptions. For example, it may be helpful to develop all the criteria information for, say, eight countries in a world region, to determine regional priorities; a second comparison might compare only the top few countries in each region against the top few in other regions to provide strategic guidance on global priorities. A firm seeking to utilize cheaper labor for product manufacture might adopt this approach using criteria such as labor rates as well as quality standards, proximity to materials, proximity to market, currency controls and local labor laws, while another company may wish only to target and prioritize its key markets.

Strategy audit

Significant added value arises in the use of the WRAP process as an approach to strategy audit for corporations that already have fairly extensive experience in working internationally. Times, circumstances and markets change, sometimes slowly, sometimes suddenly, and it is critical that major corporations continuously maximize leverage on their global positioning. Shareholder value and corporate gain intrinsic to strategic development erode over time, and although tactical and operational changes implemented by management as a response to observed change in circumstances can act to alleviate this erosion, eventually strategies need to be reviewed.

This can work in both directions. Sometimes an adopted strategy can be so successful that the company soars into a position of dominance or relative strength in its sector. Boxers become world champions but are regularly required to defend their titles; at some point almost all of them lose. Dominant and successful companies are also required to defend their position, yet can easily become blinded by their own perceived strength and unable to comprehend their weaknesses before it is almost or actually too late. Examples abound of firms that once ruled their planet and are now consigned to sources of archive material for business historians and academics. What ever happened to Pan American, or Hitachi Seiki, and countless others whose names were once spoken with reverence? What is happening now to the Polaroid Corporation? And what about British Airways, whose focus on comfortable travel at premium rates targeted on the US market fell apart during the recession of the 1990s, and whose profits have yet to recover as it struggles to compete with no-frills airlines?

On the other hand, there are many companies that implement less successful or less ambitious strategies. Strategy fails for a number of reasons, of which the most common are probably:–

- The strategy is poorly or inadequately researched and fails to properly take account of competitive challenges and international market and financial realities

- It is poorly or inadequately implemented, lacking sufficient management time or financial resources, or becomes de-focused through internal politics, obsession with short-term opportunism, or other reasons.

The results of strategy implementation may show improvement in a company's overall performance simply because there is more focus than previously existed in the company. However, a degree of improvement is achievable through many channels, and the purpose of a strategy is to prioritize opportunity and manage risk in a focused and informed way to maximize shareholder benefit. Strategies that fail can also do almost irreparable harm to a company's prospects, not only by wasting valuable resources on objectives that are unachievable in the chosen approach, but also by misdirecting the company (and its shareholders) in its operations over the period during which the strategy was being implemented.

Events, contextual change, competitive response, new technologies, and a host of other issues need to be taken into account if dominance and success are to be maintained. That is part of the job of the board, to ensure that its corporate strategy remains capable of ensuring company survival in the face of chance or deliberate challenge, and that the investment risks taken by shareholders are continually addressed.

Strategies for complex organizations such as conglomerate corporations, with their typical emphasis on building shareholder value through more effective utilization of resources and leaving operational objectives to individual subsidiaries, are often more open to risk at lower levels. This is often perceived as being counterbalanced by investment in a spread of sectors and a mixture of 'cash cow' and developmental subsidiaries. But this leverage can easily be put out of balance as markets, currency exchange rates, trading conditions and managements change. It is not unknown for subsidiaries perceived as cash cows (companies that require little investment but provide regular and substantial returns) to turn into dogs (companies that require continuing investment to maintain corporate life), thus destroying a holding company strategy that may be reliant on income from its subsidiaries to fund new acquisitions and developments, not to mention corporate profits and shareholder returns.

It therefore makes sense to undertake occasional strategy audits, to ensure that the strategy can adapt to changing circumstances and to review change in the contextual environment. This can be achieved with relative speed using the WRAP process, as analysis of comparative information is intrinsic to it. There are two aspects of this issue that can most easily be addressed. The first is a process of reviewing the original strategy objectives and criteria used to ensure that they remain valid and critical, while the second is concerned with reviewing changes in the contextual environment. Unless a company is very small, typically a strategy that is developed and implemented in year 1 will begin to show results in year 2, with its full evolution appearing over the following few years. The only predictable situation that will arise over that period is that some things will indeed change; in fact, it is imperative that change take its place beside death and taxes as one of the only reliable facets of life left in the modern world. It is wise management of risk and opportunity to be aware of the potential effect on a company's strategy of trends most likely to have a major effect on developments in sectors of primary interest to the organization.

Figure 7.7   Ten Recent Strategy-Killing Events

1. Early 1990s recession in western Europe leads to bankruptcies, mergers and financial restructuring
2. Destruction of World Trade Center twin towers in New York causes loss of confidence in US economy and slowdown in world trade
3. Mid 1990s slowdown and recessions in Japan and east Asian tiger economies
4. Terrorist attack on tourists in Luxor destroys vital Egyptian tourist business
5. Collapse of European communist regimes and access to cheaper labor causes manufacturing shift to central and eastern Europe
6. Gradual opening of Chinese economy leads to major shifts in manufacturing industry to that territory, accelerating sector decline in traditional manufacturing countries
7. Medical needs of an ageing population puts pressure on healthcare funding systems in western Europe
8. Large decline in international value of US dollar currency
9. Enron scandal in the US destroys major global accounting firm
10. Russian economy begins to revive

Strategy is essentially about priorities within a greater corporate vision of the world. When, for any reason, the circumstances underpinning the corporate vision begin to alter, the priorities supporting the achievement of that vision also need to be rethought. For example, a company that supplies machinery to manufacturing industry may be looking to change its priority target markets from Europe to China, but plans to continue to supply the same sector. Centers of production may also shift to developing markets, while the corporate vision remains essentially the same. Change is an inherent aspect of business life at all levels, but most particularly at the strategic level. While sensible managements do review their strategies to some degree, many of the changes that affect strategic developments can in fact be identified at an earlier stage through more systematic monitoring of the strategic position.

Figure 7.8   The South East Asia Bubble

A large manufacturing corporation based in Europe supplied its products on a global scale with sales and distribution undertaken by distributors located in every territory served. Over the years the company was relatively successful, but the time came when the sector that it supplied began to exhibit signs of slowdown in its purchases. The rate of slowdown was patchy, with some countries showing continuing growth, and the board determined that the time had come to revisit their strategy and review its priorities.

The first problem that arose was that the company's priorities were based not on market potential but on the volume of sales to their distributors, and an annual percentage increase in sales was negotiated according to the market information supplied by each distributor. This resulted in a range of corporate assumptions about their strengths, weaknesses and risks in which the popularity of their product range, matched by levels of sales, was much stronger in Chile than Brazil and Argentina; Switzerland and Finland were star European performers, and Singapore dominated east Asian sales. Investigating further, the company discovered that their own independent global market information was too weak to actually determine what their priorities should be. The WRAP process was invoked with three simple instructions:-

• Identify the largest worldwide markets for our products
• Determine the priority markets
• Develop a strategy for target market development

Allowing for obvious and knowledge-based exclusions, around 60 countries in five regions were reviewed and market information developed and compared for each. It was found that although some individual countries held larger markets, as a region east Asia held the most potential for market development, in particular in the tiger economies. A strategy was developed that when implemented would significantly increase the company's market share in the region through resourcing and managing operations in the prioritized territories. This growth would provide sufficient impact over a period on overall profitability to allow scope for increasing shareholder dividends, which had remained static for some time, as well as to fund developments in other major markets.

Just after the strategy was agreed with the board the Asian economies sank into downturn and recession. The strategy was shelved until brighter times arrived, when it could be suitably refined, updated and implemented. By that time, the Chinese market had grown so much that it outstripped all the other target territories in the region and thus itself became the single major priority market. The Asian strategy remains shelved and the China strategy has yet to be fully developed. Surely a case for a strategy audit?

8
Routes to Market

The question of routes to market encompasses issues around operating within the constraints of the organization's field of endeavor. In other words, the nature of the terrain has been established through market assessment, and the organization's own capabilities are better understood, and it is therefore possible to make decisions about modes of operation in the market. And operation requires, in some form, the presence to make it effective.

What is presence?

In a global strategic context, market presence equates to the level of visible organizational activity within a territory or region. This can encompass anything from a unadvertised but accessible web site, to a low-level sales and marketing operation managed in-country by a local agent, through to a full-scale manufacturing subsidiary supporting high-profile direct sales activity throughout an entire region.

In short, the concept of presence is built upon the age-old fact of life that, beyond actually doing some particular thing and even doing it well, it is useful to be seen to be doing it in such a way as to leave a memorable impression and attract further attention to the enterprise. A higher level of market presence also supplies opportunities for regular, direct and active observation of the market and sets the stage for a closer understanding of the market in the long term, allowing the accumulation of a corporate base of knowledge that can be further leveraged as developments within the market permit. In this way presence is used to both fulfil and maximize opportunity by promoting a focused approach to key markets.

Degree of presence is not necessarily tied to a specific route to market. It is possible to maintain a high profile through a website that does not translate into physical infrastructure in the form of a retail establishment. Similarly for some organizations with a comprehensive global presence even a direct sales operation in a small market can function as a low-key presence that keeps the organization's name ticking over in that territory. Appropriate levels of presence depend on the strategic objectives of the organization.

The need for presence arises from many sources. On the most obvious level, sustained market presence provides visibility to the customer base and allows the development of a broad range of national contacts amongst both the customer and supplier base, and these relationships can be expanded and deepened over time. Beyond this, it is also of practical benefit to take the time to identify and cultivate opinion leaders or other influential individuals or organizations in the marketplace. Whether such opinion leaders are willing or able to endorse products or organizations is generally an individual matter, but in any case their local awareness can make them valuable barometers of market conditions.

This leads into the wider issue of maintaining and enhancing local market and competitor information in a systematic way. It is reasonable to assume that market characteristics can and will change over time, and these changes can most effectively be tracked and potentially anticipated and appropriate responses put in place through a market monitoring program which relies in part on direct market feedback. Through direct presence it is easier not only to monitor customer demand and product or service preferences but to elucidate the motivations behind these preferences, giving the organization an improved chance of avoiding long-term stagnation.

Promotion of the organization and its product offerings may, depending on the market segment, benefit strongly from focus on the local market through demonstrating responsiveness to customer needs and desires. Increased presence enhances the ability to proactively manage the market, possibly through identifying opportunities for expansion or extension to new or more profitable products and services, or through identifying the appropriate moment to reduce presence in a contracting market. It also enables a more direct grip on quality control issues, whether these relate to product functionality or to issues of logistics and customer service and support.

One of the most important but least appreciated aspects of market presence is as a show of commitment to a territory in which the organization determines to operate. To paraphrase the proverb, one highly visible action is worth a thousand fine words. A high-profile market presence can suggest a serious and long-term commitment to the customer base, whether this is perceived in terms of understanding its unique requirements or maintaining the capability to provide appropriate service and support arrangements to the local market. Presence can, in this case, provide a sense of security by both enhancing organizational credibility and increasing the customers' level of comfort with the organization and its offerings.

It will be noticed that these comments are based on the idea that any degree of deliberate, rather than fortuitous, market presence naturally assumes that some type of market prioritization has already been put in place. Once the organization has a practical awareness of what is actually achievable and consequent priorities have been identified, it is possible to assess how best the territories or regions in question can be accessed and exploited to the desired degree. In other words, it becomes possible to outline pragmatic routes to market. Although there may seem to be a vast range of ways to accomplish market access, in practice the necessary level of market presence will be delimited by determining what is required to fulfil corporate objectives in prioritized markets.

Looked at from this perspective, level of presence depends on ambitions in the marketplace. In markets that have been determined to be of lesser importance to the achievement of organizational objectives, it may well suffice to maintain minimal presence through basic promotional activities managed from outside the territory, or through the utilization of an agent, distributor or wholesaler enjoying a minimal level of support from the home office. High-priority territories, in which the organization has defined strategic ambitions, are likely to merit a more active and up-front presence in support of such goals. It should be noted, however, that some governments in effect predefine the level of presence available by requiring foreign companies to work only with local partners, whether individual agents, corporate entities or state enterprises, and to adopt only a secondary role in the partnership.

It can indeed be argued that dominance requires visibility: if the corporate objective is to be the global market leader or the leader in a given territory, this will not be achieved in secret. This does not necessarily mean making the organization a household name, but ensuring that the defined customer base is, at some level, aware of the company and its products and services and has appropriate access to them. A very visible presence on its own is not a guarantee of market dominance, but it is crucial in bringing to public attention the efforts made in information development, product placement, and pricing. The quest for dominance and visibility must also be balanced against the organization's ability and willingness to engage with competitors. The development of a strong presence in a selected market can be interpreted as an aggressive move designed to challenge or provoke existing participants and gain market share. At the stage of market assessment the competitive environment will have been taken into account, and this is likely at the very least to have identified key competitors and their strengths and weaknesses, and assessed their ability to respond to any new threat to their market position. Of course, it is rare that such responses can be outlined with absolute certainty, but it is important that the organization has at least some awareness of what to expect from the competition in order to provide an adequate challenge to existing market dominance.

Reaching the market

The issue of trade barriers, or barriers to entry, is generally considered to be fundamental to any discussion of potential routes to market. Barriers to entry to foreign markets are traditionally defined as any situation that either prohibits or impedes access to a market. Such barriers are acknowledged to be difficult or in some cases impossible to overcome, and to be permanently present even after an organization has made inroads into the market.

In our view, this is a potentially misleading approach to foreign markets. Barriers to entry do exist, but it is more useful to distinguish between two very different types of barrier. True external barriers to trade place an absolute restriction on an organization's ability to do business in a specific territory for reasons that are external to the company's product or service offering. Operational barriers are limitations to trade that arise as a result of the company's product or service offering or mode of supply being in some way unsuited to the market and therefore actively rejected by prospective customers.

It is crucial to make a distinction between external barriers to entry and barriers that are created by the organization itself by such means as taking an inappropriate approach to the market, or by offering products or services that are not appropriate to the market. Operational barriers can often be ameliorated or perhaps entirely removed through judicious investment in skills or staff, or by a more thoughtful and responsive approach. In some cases, it may be appropriate to accept their existence as an indication that a national market is unsuitable or inherently difficult given the products or services that a company has to offer, and subsequently focus development efforts elsewhere. By contrast, external barriers are firm, and are not amenable to short-term alteration or manipulation.

Organizations affected by such barriers can of course lobby for their change or repeal, or conduct public relations campaigns intended to change the prevailing point of view, but until any change is implemented the organization is effectively constrained in its market participation.

Recognizing and being prepared to address operational barriers is a key aspect of market prioritization. If barriers are capable of being overcome through investment, it is critical to know what level of investment might be repaid through market entry.

External barriers

There are very few genuine external barriers to trade in most places that pose insuperable obstacles to market entry. These are almost always related to some aspect of the relationship between sovereign states, rather than to the essential business relationship between supplier and customer. Those barriers that do indiscriminately restrict market participation are summarized below:-

Legal barriers. Legal barriers may prohibit the supply of specific goods and services to certain countries, or alternately a blanket prohibition may exist preventing organizations from dealing with a specific territory in any capacity. In either case the effect of a legal barrier is to prohibit rather than restrict the supply of goods or services into a given territory.

Such barriers are by definition made operative by governments for reasons that may or may not be related to competitive issues. Defense and security industries in the major defense equipment territories are widely subject to legal barriers that prohibit the supply of armaments or any type of related equipment to certain governments, either for security or humanitarian reasons. However, other industries are not immune from the imposition of such barriers, with various foodstuffs in particular often subject to restrictions on international trade due to public health issues or trade quota systems. Many of these restrictive practices relate to domestic employment needs, such as the US ban on imports of cotton, while others are more closely directed at maintaining high market price levels for commodity products within, for example, the European Union.

Legal barriers very often have direct political ramifications, as in the sanctions against Iraq that were operative during the 1990s and beyond, and which were ultimately intended to achieve the political end of hastening the demise of a regime by withholding essential industrial and consumer supplies to the territory. US legal barriers to trade with Cuba are a similar example of an existing blanket prohibition.

Legal barriers to trade can also take the form of 'required content' legislation that demands that certain industry sectors limit the content of their product or service to domestic suppliers only. For example, this is particularly significant within the U.S. defense market, in which contractors may be required to source all components from U.S.-based companies only. This restriction is ostensibly intended to protect the national security interests by eliminating any reliance on foreign contractors for the development or manufacture of key defense products. However, it is important to note that this barrier itself may in certain cases be managed through judicious acquisition of appropriate domestic firms capable of servicing critical market demand, or by establishing a production facility in the US to serve the market directly.

Tariffs. The imposition of tariffs by one nation against particular goods or services, or against particular countries, is generally intended to restrict or penalize a specific aspect of trade with a view to aiding domestic industry, rather than to eliminate this trade permanently. Nevertheless, tariffs pose an effective barrier to trade by artificially raising the price of a given good or service to such a degree that it becomes difficult or perhaps impossible for foreign companies to compete with domestic producers. India used to provide many examples of high tariffs for imported products, up to 50 per cent in some cases, but in the last decade its markets have become much more open and this territory is now experiencing economic growth rates of over 7 per cent annually.

A possible, although viciously expensive response to tariff-induced barriers to trade is to take the decision to hold out: if this means supplying goods at less than cost over a prolonged period, so be it, as long as this approach supports the organization's long-term position of maintaining a significant market presence. Unfortunately, even if an organization is financially and conceptually capable of carrying out this challenge it may be perceived to be 'dumping' goods in a foreign market, thus sparking retaliation against its home territory or industry, possibly with the blessings of the World Trade Organization. Tariff barriers are not impermeable in the same way as legal barriers as they can be changed much more quickly, but there are few ways in which an organization can work to mitigate their effects in the immediate term.

Boycotts. In this context, boycotts to supply refer to instances when there is a large-scale rejection of goods or services by the customer base in a territory on the basis of some characteristic that is external to the product itself and the means by which it is supplied. In other words, the product and its route to market are themselves acceptable, but some aspect of the supplier or its home territory have become unacceptable to the end-user, who acts out this rejection through a boycott of the product in question. Boycotts have no legal status, but they can effectively close the market to certain products or suppliers until customer perception changes. A well-known example of effective boycotting occurred some years ago when goods from the apartheid regime in South Africa, including fruit and wine, were simply not purchased in any volume over a period of years in some of its key markets such as the UK and other European countries. This, allied to other economic sanctions, was so effective that the value of the rand declined heavily and helped to mark the end of the regime itself.

Boycotts are primarily related to what may be broadly deemed 'political' circumstances. Such a boycott may be motivated by direct political developments, or by environmental, social, economic, or other humanitarian issues that galvanize a group of end-users to reject a product or service in response to an issue external to the product.

Operational barriers

In contrast to external barriers, operational barriers to entry refer to barriers that are created by an organization's inappropriate approach to a specific market and its end-user base, which effectively motivates the potential customer base to reject the product or service on offer. Paradoxically, these are the issues that most commentators refer to when they wish to discuss 'trade barriers' between nations: they are the cultural, social, or supply-related issues that discourage end-users from purchasing the product or dealing with the company because in some way this does not meet their varied needs or desires. This situation arises in turn because, in many cases, suppliers have failed to properly understand the requirements of their foreign customer base.

Operational barriers are much more fluid than external barriers and can in many cases be overcome, provided the organization possesses the will and the resources to recognize and address these barriers. Significantly, this in turn is likely to depend on the potential of the market to fulfil organizational objectives. If efforts to overcome operational barriers are too costly compared to market potential, corporate objectives may not be adequately met.

For example, it may be the case that the organization forgoes altering its product or service to make it more acceptable to the market because it does not believe that doing so would be worthwhile. This may be because the cost of product or service alteration would be prohibitive compared to the benefit gained, or because the organization believes that the basic product or service may be offered successfully in a range of alternate markets that are of more value to organizational objectives than those markets in which the product is not immediately acceptable.

In this context, operational barriers to trade to include perceived historical or cultural barriers to the acceptance of products. This can encompass genuine cultural barriers to acceptability, such as an absolute unwillingness to consume pork products in predominantly Muslim and Jewish territories (and indeed, in some countries this can become a legal barrier). Alternately, it may describe a cultural issue that is much more nebulous and correspondingly difficult to verify. These include the types of 'barriers' that have been described by managers, such as 'The French generally dislike the English and won't do business with them,' or 'German industries operate cartels and deliberately exclude foreign companies from participating in the market'. Experience suggests that these situations are in practice quite rare, and have much more to do with the attitude and approach of the foreign company than with any real antagonism on the part of the nationalities concerned. In practice, everyone in the commercial world wants to do business in a manner advantageous to themselves, and learning how to do business with them is simply a preliminary aspect to accessing international markets.

The benefits of thinking in terms of external versus operational barriers are twofold. It allows the management to distinguish those circumstances that are amenable to influence from those that are inflexible, permitting a more realistic allocation of resources supporting and extending presence in non-domestic markets. It also encourages managers to think constructively and creatively in terms of how to assess and serve markets, rather than simply attributing their weakness in the marketplace to trade barriers.

Supply chain

A major prerequisite for getting to grips with customer motivation in non-domestic markets is an awareness of the structure of the supply chain in the target market. This entails an understanding of where and how an organization can fit into the supply chain, as well as where customers are placed in the chain and how their own requirements influence the market.

It may be useful at this point to briefly review a schematic outline (Figure 8.1) of the supply chain which could equally be applied to domestic or non-domestic markets. The basis of the supply chain is, in terms of product-based industries, the manufacturer or originator. The finished products may be sold directly to the end-user, or sold to a distributor or wholesaler responsible for managing product supply to an entire territory or to a defined region within the territory. Distributors providing coverage for an entire national territory may in turn contract with sub-distributors in various regions where, for example, their contact base is weaker or where there are specific cultural, linguistic, or logistic reasons for employing a third party with greater local capabilities. In consumer-focused markets the distributor or wholesaler is likely to use retailers offering the sales outlets and marketing skills to bring the product to public attention. In many cases, particularly consumer markets, the end-user sits at the end of the supply chain.

There's nothing new or startling in this short description of the road from producer to consumer. What is less commonly appreciated is the chain of influence that works through the supply chain. The chain of influence is made up of the pressures placed on each component of the supply chain by those elements further up and down the chain, and by the responses to these pressures manifested by each participant in the chain. In practice, the straightforward supply chain within a particular industry may operate in very similar ways in different national markets. However, the chain of influence within that supply chain may vary subtly, or possibly significantly, from the one that obtains in the domestic market.

This suggests that there are likely to be at least two, if not more, constituencies to satisfy (distributor and customer) in order to make headway in a foreign market, often without being able to exert the level of control or influence an organization might expect to wield in the domestic market. The existence of a chain of influence indicates that it is critical to differentiate between the various types of buyer encountered on the way to the end-user. Each of them will have their

Figure 8.1   The Supply Chain in Outline

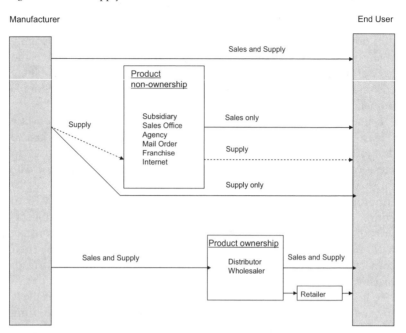

own criteria for judging the product, their own requirements to fulfil, and their own reasons for adopting (or not) the item on offer to them.

Furthermore, it is also useful to consider what types of customer are present in the territory and why they are there, which may have a profound effect on the way in which they should best be approached. Is the end-user base made up primarily of domestic companies, or is there a significant base of foreign-owned enterprises operating in the territory? Crucially, this may impact on access to the relevant procurement organizations, which in practice might not be where they are assumed to be. This situation can be observed in the automotive industry. The global automotive manufacturers often have assembly plants in several countries on different continents, which are served by both global first-tier suppliers and smaller domestic suppliers and subcontractors. In this situation a German-owned original equipment manufacturer (OEM) in Spain, for example, is likely to have its own procurement system in place, but actual purchasing decisions are often heavily influenced or even directed by corporate head office. In some cases this extends as far as specifying the equipment that suppliers must use in the manufacturing process.

This in turn suggests that the shape of the supply chain may have a direct effect on market prioritization. In the scenario just mentioned an automotive supplier would find it useful to take into account that purchasing decisions taken in Spain are effectively driven from Germany, indicating that market development focused on Germany and its domestic companies may in practice show results in other markets.

Beyond the formal supply chain, the chain of influence also encompasses those additional constituencies that exercise an important influence over the acquisition and use of products or services. Although such individuals or organizations generally do not purchase the products themselves, and have no direct authority or influence over procurement practices, they may well have a critical impact on the way the product is received by the end-user base or by the wider public that perceives itself to be affected by the deployment of the product or service in question.

These influencers may become particularly important in foreign markets due to their unexpected impact on the organization's ability to sell product, either in a specific territory or globally. Since the influencers do not buy the product themselves they do not stimulate a direct boycott, but pressure exerted through interest groups or media outlets may operate to make the market position untenable. This aspect of the chain of influence can depict a crossover between business-to-business and consumer sectors: products not marketed to consumers can still be perceived by them to have wider social, environmental, or economic consequences that the supplier must take into account.

Routes to market: establishing presence

Indirect presence

Indirect presence describes the effort to gain a degree of market access without establishing physical presence in the market. This may be a useful approach in the case of lower-priority markets, in which conditions indicate that major investment will not be productive in achieving corporate objectives. It may also be expected to generate some sales in such markets, maintaining the organization's profile as a minor participant without demanding undue attention or resources. Indirect presence may be also used as a wide-ranging public relations tool, offering the suggestion of a wider or more well-established presence than the organization actually commands.

Advertising, direct mail, or similar activities can be used in an effort to gain market presence without engaging in direct activity in a territory. This often comes into play in cases where organizations advertise in regional trade publications, perhaps covering the whole of Europe or Southeast Asia, without deliberately intending to service every territory in that region. This does offer a basic regional presence that can be extended over time as the organization becomes established in core territories.

However, the use of indirect presence raises two immediate problems, both related to the organization's actual ability to service potential customers across a disparate range of territories. It must first be logistically feasible to bring products or services to the market; that is, potential customers must actually be able to get their hands on products without undue delay or difficulty. Secondly, customer service and support issues must be addressed before any supply is made, as a means of ensuring that failure in this area does not ultimately jeopardize the organization's longer-term potential and ambitions in the market.

The concept of indirect market presence has become much more important since the advent of the most basic form of presence in the modern global economy, the ubiquitous and practically indispensable website. The fact that the website is accessible to anyone in the world with an internet connection allows it to fulfil its minimal function as reference for the organization, always provided the relevant customer base has the ability and the will to take a look at the site in the first place.

Although this is not the appropriate forum for an extended dissertation on e-commerce in the global marketplace, it is worthwhile taking a brief look at what can and can't be achieved with an internet presence alone. A website can provide corporate information such as financial data, technical specifications, distributor lists, management biographies, or myriad additional details that serve to ground the organization in reality and promote its capabilities and track record to a worldwide audience. It can function as a portal for customer-specific e-business services such as order tracking that would otherwise be provided by individuals through traditional communication channels such as post or telephone, or possibly not provided at all. It can offer information to the general public on relevant topics as a combined community service and public relations exercise. Not least, it can even be used to sell products or to provide services in innovative ways.

A website can enhance market presence, and can be leveraged to extend it to new territories, but it cannot replace market presence entirely. It is not the universal panacea for those organizations that do not want to spend the time and money learning about their markets and becoming properly established in them. Of course it happens from time to time that companies receive enquiries or even orders from customers thousands of miles away who know the company only through its website. These should be treated like any other enquiry: if they can be managed without distracting too much attention from priority markets, then all well and good, but chasing random opportunities from any source should not in itself become the focus of a business with global ambitions.

It may be objected at this point that e-commerce is entirely about *not* maintaining an unnecessary physical infrastructure, even in priority markets, and therefore the issue of presence is becoming superfluous in the wake of this new technological paradigm. This would be to misunderstand the nature of market presence and what it is intended to achieve. Maintaining a focused market presence is a two-way street: it offers the customer base the comfort of knowing that the company is interested in them for the long term and committed to serving them without suddenly disappearing or losing interest in the market, and it allows the organization itself to learn, developing its offerings in response to changes on the ground.

In practice, websites can be, and are, used to provide and project direct presence in a specific market. Amazon.com, now the internet's largest bookseller, operates sites specific to the US, Canadian, UK, French, German, and Japanese markets, allowing the online retailer to target the customer base with products of specific interest in recognizable currencies, with logistics and delivery backup designed to address the specific requirements of the territory. Of course, there is nothing to prevent a Brazilian shopper from logging on to pick up the new edition of *Canadian History for Dummies*, but they will need to wait patiently, and pay good money for, delivery to a location that does not figure as one of the business's core territories.

Again, it may be objected that presence on the internet can function as a portal to a niche customer base that is geographically widespread and not defined by any specific national or cultural issues. This may indeed be the case in situations in which the customer base for an e-commerce offering is highly diverse, or where an e-business portal is provided to private or public-sector customers across a range of national territories. It is nevertheless the case that, in these circumstances, legal, cultural, and market-specific issues must be acknowledged and monitored in order to ensure that unity in diversity does not fragment due to unsuspected and unrecognized fractures in the customer base.

Distributors and agents

The use of distributors and agents in non-domestic markets is perhaps the most common means of gaining access to the global marketplace, particularly for small to medium-sized companies or for large companies operating in non-priority markets. Although the distinction may operate at times as more a matter of semantics than actual fact, a distributor is generally accepted to be an independent entity that purchases and holds stock that is subsequently sold on to customers. An agent essentially functions as an autonomous sales representative, possibly working on commission, facilitating contact between the organization and its customer base in the territory.

The principle advantage of distributors and agents is their ability to provide a means of stable market presence without committing resources to a more risky direct investment in the territory. The advice generally handed out to companies new to international business by government trade bodies and export promotion agencies almost always includes the directive to 'get a good distributor'. In practice this piece of advice is less than helpful, as the organization may find it difficult to make sound judgments about what constitutes a good foreign distributor, or what can be done to improve a situation that is not operating according to plan.

In brief, a competent distributor should possess a good awareness of the organization's target customer base, which includes access to those customers and, where appropriate or indeed necessary, the personal contacts to guarantee that access. Where appropriate, these representatives may also be the focus for customer service and after-sales support in the local market. Their location in the country and familiarity with the market should also give them particular insight into its operation, which can be drawn in to further inform the organization's own base of information on the territory.

So far the question of securing a skilled and credible non-domestic distributor seems quite straightforward, but the relationship is often much more complex than is generally appreciated and often requires more active management than the organization expects. The assumption amongst many managers is that foreign distributors by their nature have an inbuilt incentive to sell as many units as possible of Product X at the highest price obtainable. Doesn't this simply stand to reason? As the argument goes, the distributor will naturally seek to maximize returns by pushing the product as diligently as possible, and therefore systematic monitoring of distributor performance is essentially a superfluous activity. Let us look again at the dynamic involved in this relationship. In practice, distributors have their own strategies and agendas, which may be quite distinct from those of their principals. This is logical, rational, and not at all surprising. After all, they are running a business of which the product offering of one of their principals is likely to form only a limited part. Consequently the distributor will be concerned with a range of issues, and possibly with a range of markets, that may be of only peripheral interest to an individual manager in terms of getting their own product to market.

One of the most common mistakes in international business is to become entirely dependent on distributors and their strategies without making an independent effort to comprehend the distributor's own approach to their market, or to understand the requirements of the end-user and their markets. These are two distinct issues and must be treated as such if the manager is to develop a full picture of the market and understand the relationships within it. This is, indeed, why we have treated the issues of foreign customers, cultures, and routes to market in such detail, for a global strategy is effectively baseless without taking into account these issues that shape the environment in which the organization is required to operate.

Let us now examine the approach to business of a hypothetical distributor. For simplicity's sake, we'll assume that the distributor is selling only two products, the organization's own (Product A) and a complementary product (Product B) that is sold to a broadly similar range of end-users, but does not compete directly with Product A. We will also assume that Product A is inexpensive and appeals to a wider range of end-users, while Product B is relatively costly and also more likely to be of interest to a specialist or niche segment of the market. From the distributor's point of view, they now have a reasonably balanced portfolio, giving them potential access to a wider spectrum of customers throughout the market: where one product is inappropriate, the other might find a buyer.

Just to make the situation more complicated and interesting, we will add another simple variable: profit margin. Product B is something of a challenge to sell, being a costly item with a smaller base of potential customers, but the significant margin makes it worthwhile for the distributor's salespeople to push it hard, falling back on the more basic Product A only when they have no chance of making the higher-margin sale.

In an alternate scenario, the distributor may find that Product B is easier to shift for a whole raft of reasons: it's stylish, high-tech, durable, easy to use, or German. Although the margins are roughly the same, the relative ease and speed with which Product B can be sold makes it more attractive to the sales force, who in any case are essentially interested in earning a good living from selling products that do not haunt them with service or suitability issues further down the line. In either case, Product A is failing to sell not necessarily because it is unsuited to the market, but because it compares unfavorably in some respect to other products in the distributor's portfolio which can be sold with greater ease and/or more profit. This is in many cases the first competitive challenge that must be overcome in order to adequately access the market.

These dilemmas can be exacerbated if the organization is dealing with a distributor that is itself very large or highly diverse, and which will therefore operate within a strategic context far wider than its direct interest in one principal and its product lines. This type of sales and marketing organization can be particularly prevalent in developing countries, where a distributor might spread its interests by dealing in widely differentiated sectors that are initially relatively small, but show potential for significant growth. This is not to suggest that such distributors are in any way unresponsive or less effective; indeed, their wide range of interests in the territory may offer unexpected benefits in terms of market access by giving them broad awareness of the way in which various market sectors are likely to develop over time. At the same time, it is also necessary to realize that strategic considerations for such a company must encompass far more than the interests of any single organization that the distributor happens to represent in the territory.

These observations are not intended to provoke mistrust and discord between distributors and their principals, or to generate suspicion as to the motives of the various parties involved in the supply chain. Naturally, it makes sense to work together to achieve common goals, and in the process of doing this it is mature and realistic to recognize that everyone's aims may not be identical at all times. This is why independent market awareness and distributor monitoring becomes such a critical aspect of managing non-domestic business: it is a tool that ensures that an organization's objectives are being served adequately by the agent or distributor, and if not, it provides a means of bringing the two sets of objectives back into line. It also helps to explain why information is such a

Figure 8.2 The Italian Job

Distributor management and monitoring is critical to ensuring that the organization performs according to informed expectations in a non-domestic market. However, there may come a point at which it becomes evident that the interests of the distributor and the principal diverge so significantly that the relationship may need to be entirely re-evaluated.

A UK-based engineering manufacturing company had become so concerned about what it considered to be poor sales performance in the Italian market that it contemplated pulling out of the territory altogether. A focused re-assessment of European markets, however, indicated that Italy should be a major market for the organization's products. Furthermore, Italy's position as a key industrial economy made wholesale abandonment of the territory conceptually difficult, as it would deal a serious blow to the organization's claim to global leadership in its market segments. Why should increasing sales be so difficult?

The organization was represented in Italy by a distributor offering a portfolio of equipment balanced according to the requirements of the Italian engineering sector. The distributor expected approximately 30-40 per cent of his revenues to be provided by specialist, high-margin products, another 30-40 per cent to come from high-volume products of the type supplied by his UK principal, and the remainder to come from a diverse range of products not directly competitive with his key principals. As the distributor saw it, he was well represented at various levels of the market, and investment of further resources in one market segment would unbalance the portfolio, making his company overly dependent on one part of the market and running the risk of losing focus on other important segments. Although the distributor was keen to maintain the relationship with the UK organization his main interest, and indeed responsibility, was the sound management of his own organization.

What's a principal to do? In this case, the best way for the organization to increase volume sales was likely to be through the establishment of a direct sales organization wholly focused on the company's products. Leaving the distributor was a risk, as this company had an excellent reputation in the market and could find ways to retaliate against a new competitor, but it was likely that sales would remain constrained under these circumstances. Where should the priority lie?

critical part of strategy development: without it, as demonstrated in Figure 8.2, there is little basis for understanding or making sound judgments about the dynamics of the supply chain.

Ultimately the most productive approach is to work in partnership with the distributor or agent, rather than in a relationship of dependence. Effective partnerships in turn require constructive management of the distributor relationship so that expectations and responsibilities are clear on both sides. From this it follows that a certain amount of independent information and ongoing feedback is necessary for the organization to understand its own position in the local market. This makes it possible to put together a coherent and well-informed plan of action for attacking the market, and enables longer-term monitoring of distributor performance.

Once again, how extensive this process ought to be in global terms is dependent on corporate priorities. In non-priority territories, it is quite reasonable to organize a relationship with a local distributor and leave them to tick over peacefully, providing local presence with minimal investment, as in the Peruvian experiment in Chapter 1. This frees up effort and resources for focused development of priority markets.

Licensing

The licensing of income-generating activities in the foreign market offers a means of market entry by making use of another organization's existing facilities, which may include R&D, production, or sales and marketing facilities, in the target market without engaging in direct presence. This can include the licensing of IPRs to a third party, who may then utilize the technology in the manufacture of products appropriate to the market. Alternately, the right to manufacture specific products or utilize proprietary technologies may be licensed in a territory in which the products may either find a reasonable market, or from which they may be profitably exported to a third territory.

The use of licensing presupposes an adequate assessment of the legal issues, particularly those surrounding intellectual property and the enforcement of corresponding rights that are obtained in the selected market. There may also be a debate about the branding or promotion of the manufactured product, and it should be clear from the outset whether the principal or the contracting company is putting their name to the finished product. If financial and IPR protection is reliable, licensing can offer a means of market access that does not demand substantial investment in direct presence, but can generate both profits and potentially a level of secondary presence that provides the organization with a preliminary profile in the target market.

Piggy-backing

'Piggy-backing' is the cheerfully descriptive name for the process of utilizing an existing opportunity as a base for developing extended market presence. This may be the result of an existing customer conducting business in another territory and using the organization as a supplier or contractor. This gives the organization an opportunity to experience the territory first-hand and to build business on the basis of awareness gained in this context. Depending on circumstances it may also give the organization a minor presence in the market in association with the customer, and in some cases it may in fact be possible to make judicious use of the customer's contacts or associates in the market as a springboard for developing its own presence.

The essence of piggy-backing is that the organization takes advantage of resources already allocated to a market in order to further its presence in the territory. This approach can function as an intermediary position between indirect and direct market presence. Although the organization is not 'officially' directly represented in the market, its managers and employees may develop enough of a presence to establish a basis for further expansion.

Direct presence

In a situation of direct presence, the organization itself sets up operations in some form in a territory as a means of directly managing the market. Direct presence offers a higher level of exposure and implies a stronger, more long-term commitment to the market. At the same time, the risks inherent in this exposure are greater: it requires a higher level of both initial and ongoing investment, and closing the operation down if it fails to deliver on corporate objectives is both expensive and provides highly public evidence of organizational retrenchment.

A direct sales organization, or a subsidiary, is likely to offer the greatest degree of control over the organization's activities in a foreign territory. In this case, the organization is free to pursue its own strategy and shape its own approach to the market without having to reconcile this with the requirements of distributors or partners. Sales and service staff are responsible directly to the organization and able to focus their efforts solely on its products and services. Direct access to customers, and the concomitant opportunity to maintain ongoing market awareness, can provide a competitive advantage through the ability to develop strong customer relationships and respond proactively to changes in the market. This most direct form of presence also shows an unambiguous commitment to the market. Finally, the presence of a subsidiary may also offer opportunities to develop other types of business in the longer term, for example by acting as a distributor or agent for complementary products or services.

The pitfalls of the direct approach are equally evident. The process of setting up an office and recruiting appropriate staff can be costly and time-consuming, as it will almost always require the assistance of various legal and business advisors to ensure the proper establishment of the new entity. Long-term management of a direct sales operation can be very demanding and introduces issues of organizational and cultural differentiation across territories that need to be reconciled with the organization's corporate culture and objectives. A direct presence also implies a long-term commitment to the market, which runs the risk of becoming inappropriate if the structure of the market changes significantly, or if the organization is not sufficiently flexible to recognize and respond to these changes.

For these reasons direct sales approach is generally utilized in territories that are considered to have a high priority in terms of the achievement of the organization's strategic objectives, and where it is determined that the returns available are likely to be commensurate with the resources employed. Of course, as an organization expands its global presence it may be appropriate to establish direct sales in lower-priority territories, but this will be dependent on the potential returns that can reasonably be drawn from such markets.

Joint ventures and acquisition

Some of the risks of establishing a subsidiary in a foreign market can be ameliorated through the use of a joint venture agreement. These can in practice take many forms, but they essentially entail a partnership arrangement, most usually with a domestic company or another established market participant, who is able to offer some advantage in accessing the market without competing directly with the organization's own offering. For example, they may have an existing customer base, a network of suppliers, or a range of market contacts able to facilitate sales and distribution. If they are truly experienced in dealing with the territory, they should have an awareness of the supply chain and the nature of local customer demand. They may offer a manufacturing base near to market, or have ready access to technology that is more acceptable within the market.

A sound joint venture agreement can significantly reduce the learning curve in a new market and speed the process of gaining credibility with the customer base and, ultimately, showing a profit. However, the greatest risk in entering into a joint venture is choosing a reliable partner in the first instance who is demonstrably capable of fulfilling the agreed requirements of the partnership, and who can be relied upon not to disappear with profits generated by a successful partnership.

Acquisition obviously entails the organization buying its way into a territory by acquiring an existing market participant, either an indigenous company or another non-domestic organization with an established presence in the market. This operation can then be incorporated into the parent company while offering a ready-made platform for expanding into a new market on the strength of the acquisition's contacts and customer base. An acquired company also offers the advantage of a known presence in the market and can circumvent the challenge of bringing to market entirely new products that have no recognizable brand existence in the territory.

Direct marketing

Direct marketing comprises such approaches as catalogues, direct mail, newspaper inserts, or telephone marketing that do not require a physical infrastructure to present products to the customer. Nevertheless, this form of market presence still requires a distribution structure appropriate to the territory, as well as a suitable customer service structure to handle product returns or customer complaints in an effective manner.

Although direct marketing is famed in some quarters as essentially a numbers game, more sophisticated operations do strive to target key niches in the market in order to maximize sales in a cost-effective manner and improve their opportunity to develop long-term customer relationships.

Franchising

In a franchising operation a third party buys the right to operate a business in a defined territory, agreeing to position the business in a certain manner and to maintain brand awareness in the new territory. At the same time the franchisee can expect to benefit from the publicity and marketing efforts of the parent company on a wider scale.

Franchising can remove significant risk from the franchising organization through shifting responsibility for local management on to the operator of the franchise. However, this does not completely eliminate the problem of risk, as any failure and retrenchment is likely to reflect poorly on the organization. This may in turn reflect poorly on its reputation in the home market, for example in its ability to raise finance to fund other types of expansion.

Non-domestic supply: production and outsourcing

One of the key aspects of global business development in the twenty-first century is the increased tendency to consider foreign production or outsourcing as a means of increasing the organization's competitiveness both at home and abroad. The idea is by no means a new one: in the 1980s and '90s the electronics giant Siemens was manufacturing in or outsourcing components to plants in developing countries, while final assembly was carried out in the home market in order to earn the 'Made in Germany' badge. The popularity of the concept has accelerated over the past five to ten years for many reasons. These include the increased financial, economic and political stability of many developing countries, particularly in Asia, and their concomitant enthusiasm for putting in place measures to attract foreign investment as a means of job creation and industry cluster development. The growth of end-user markets in such territories, whether consumer, business, or government, has also contributed to an increased interest in locating facilities for supply near the customer base.

The establishment of manufacturing or other supply facilities in a foreign territory may be accomplished in several ways. The most straightforward is a direct operation, in which the facility is set up and managed by the parent company and foreign workers are directly employed by this organization. Alternately, full production or supply may be outsourced or subcontracted to a firm in another territory with an established track record in the sector and with a demonstrable capability of fulfiling quality and logistic requirements. Individual components of the production process can also be outsourced to non-domestic firms providing contract manufacturing services.

Non-domestic supply of goods or services may be advocated for one of two reasons. It may offer significant cost benefits, perhaps in terms of labor rates or raw material prices, thus providing the organization with a very competitive price advantage in its traditional markets. This low-cost manufacturing facility may also be used to supply newly-developed markets in which price sensitivity is high and where production costs must be kept to a minimum in order to preserve margins and establish a competitive presence.

Foreign outsourcing is in effect an extension of the practice of outsourcing non-core activities to specialist subcontractors in the domestic market. This encompasses such activities as the manufacture of component parts of larger, finished products, the development of software and IT systems, or the outsourcing of services that can be provided remotely at a much lower cost, such as call centers.

In the first instance, the case for justifying the foreign manufacture or outsourcing of products or services must be established, principally through the identification of a financial case for moving production or sourcing abroad. Furthermore, if such a project is to have a reasonable chance of success it is essential to address quality control and delivery issues from the outset. These are perhaps the most critical problems of non-domestic supply, as it can be difficult from a potentially long distance to ensure adequate standards of either quality or delivery time. Without these the positive impact of the venture will be largely negated as any cost savings or improvements in efficiency would be offset by the costs of correcting inadequate performance and placating customers aggrieved by unprecedented failures in service quality.

Finally, addressing management and resource issues is critical to the success of a foreign production or outsourcing operation. Although it is likely that at least some local management would be put in place to handle day-to-day operations it is still necessary to allocate management resource to ensure that the facility or relationship is operating satisfactorily and is adequately integrated with the larger enterprise. At the same time it is important that this endeavor does not detract significantly from the necessary management resource assigned to ongoing business in domestic or other markets.

9
Building a Strategy

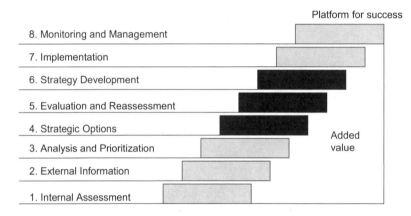

The WRAP Stairway

Platform for success

8. Monitoring and Management	
7. Implementation	
6. Strategy Development	
5. Evaluation and Reassessment	
4. Strategic Options	Added value
3. Analysis and Prioritization	
2. External Information	
1. Internal Assessment	

This chapter demonstrates the use and value of the WRAP process in building strategies that are both relevant to the company's strategic objectives and realistic in relation to the targets and priorities already determined.

The purpose of strategy is to bring sufficient focus into the activities of an organization to enable it to best achieve the objectives or goals that it desires. A corporate strategy can be understood as a prioritized set of rules or guidelines aimed at overall corporate benefit within which functional or subsidiary sub-strategies can be utilized to maximize or optimize the return on their individual sets of activities. In broad terms, most strategies fall into two categories. The first can be described as portfolio strategies dealing with a combination of widely differing business areas, and the second as competitive strategies concerned with specific business areas. Within these categories the actual strategic approach can vary dramatically. It may take the form of a prescriptive strategy, which closely defines the specific ways in which strategy development can take place. For example, a prescriptive approach may demand that all business growth take place organically, or that global expansion be driven solely by acquisition. Strategy development can also be open, making using of a process which defines the rules or guidelines for development but allows variable approaches that depend on the circumstances in which the organization operates.

The WRAP process is a means of defining priorities and does not predetermine the nature of strategies to be developed, but instead allows the required strategic concepts to evolve from its informed description of the corporation's capabilities, requirements, and priorities in an international context. It incorporates information about corporate activities, resources, culture and business style with identification of the competitive and cultural challenges that the company faces, or is

Figure 9.1 Chinese Walls

Times were tough in the engineering business and to help its members, one of the engineering trade associations devised a program in which a group of member companies would be taken through the principles of strategic marketing and assisted with the development of strategies to focus their marketing efforts in a European country. The group included both manufacturers and importers. Being members of the same trade association, their products tended to relate to a specific segment of the engineering sector and thus, in many cases, to compete with each other. This gave rise to concerns about two key issues, the first being the maintenance of absolute confidentiality of corporate information and the second on how much real differentiation there could be between strategies effectively focused on the same segment and the same buyers for the same or similar products. For the consulting firm appointed to implement this program, responding properly to the first concern was straightforward as client confidentiality is both an inbred instinct among professionals and an absolute requirement for membership of their professional institutes and associations. For the second concept of 'Chinese walls' was introduced in which that which might be spoken or discussed within the confines of the consultants' office would not be heard or acknowledged by individual consultants dealing with potentially competitive companies.

Strangely enough, this works and is probably based on the ability of the human brain to compartmentalize and file information in a little drawer marked 'not to be opened before Christmas.'. But it was ultimately unnecessary, because initial discussions with the companies found that they all held different market positions, had different objectives for the strategic program based on different sets of priorities, and operated within different corporate environments. This ensured that each strategy developed was strongly differentiated from the others, and each company could proceed to implement its own strategy to achieve its own objectives.

about to face, as it seeks to achieve its rational objectives, and thus helps to build a strong foundation for the adoption and development of bespoke strategies for each organization. In practice no two companies are the same, and although successful industry leaders often have many would-be imitators, each strategy requires to take into account a set of objectives and internal and external circumstances that is unique to the organization under scrutiny.

Wu Chi'i, who lived during the fourth century BC, was a Chinese general who also wrote a study entitled 'Art of War,' and his name and writings are often combined with those of Sun Tzu. They both deal with the principles and strategies of military warfare and essentially followed similar approaches that can be applied, with suitable adjustment, to modern international business. Wu Chi'i wrote in Chapter 1, Section 3 (Planning Operations Against Other States) of his 'Art of War', 'Now what is called the Right Way is the return to fundamental principles; righteousness is that by which affairs are advanced and merit established; planning is that by which harm is avoided and advantage gained; essentials that which safeguards one's work and protects his achievements.'.

Even allowing for the effects of translation which has produced language that may seem florid and strange, the relevance of these words to business today is as great as it was to his king in the time of Wu Chi'i. They reiterate the point that successful, actionable strategy is essentially about balance and flexibility: it takes account, insofar as possible, of each aspect of the environment that affects the organization, without becoming overly fixated on one component part of that environment or on one specific approach to addressing strategic issues. Development of the WRAP process itself has been informed by two key assumptions that we hold about strategic management:-

- Strategy needs to reflect a balance between internal competencies and external conditions as a means of determining the most effective means of achieving objectives.
- The process of strategy development itself can be generative: it can throw up new ideas and options that the organization may not have considered, primarily through the process of information development and application.

The various schools of strategic management tend to emphasize a particular aspect of the organization's environment, such as the competitive background, the corporate culture, the degree of entrepreneurship inherent in the company, or the organization's ability to learn and change, and focus on it at the expense of other elements. Our point is that in practice all these elements must be taken into account. This is nowhere more important than in global strategy development, where an unfamiliar environment gives little quarter to the strategist who chooses to ignore the relationships between capability and demand in the broadest sense. In effect, the resource that the organization is able to devote to global expansion will have different implications in different territories, and it is the responsibility of the strategist to understand the effect of these differences on corporate objectives.

It can be argued that this approach to strategic management introduces too much complexity into the process of developing a workable strategy. How can all relevant aspects of the organization and its environment be taken into account with adequate accuracy when they are so diverse? In practice, managers handle the entire gamut of corporate issues regularly; the WRAP process is simply designed to systematize the process of recognizing these issues and their influence on strategic development. Far from being overly complex, the process provides a tool for the rational organization and analysis of these issues as a means of ensuring that they are not ignored either deliberately or accidentally.

There are essentially three topics that require to be addressed and considered for the development of effective strategy: setting strategic objectives; identifying, collecting, analyzing and utilizing information and data that is relevant to the task; and determining the best approach toward achievement of the objectives within the environment described.

Within these determinations, development of a successful international strategy focuses on five key elements:-

- Corporate objectives
- Corporate resources and competencies
- Priority targets
- Business environment or context
- Business opportunity

There is an argument touched on earlier in this book that suggests that product pushing can lead to successful international business. Allied to this is the concept that a brand that is successful in a single country or region can be easily sold globally, with relatively minor changes in packaging and pricing. The reality is that this works best for strong, well-known brands from countries with a significant and well established international pedigree such as Colgate-Palmolive, Siemens, Roche Pharmaceuticals, Boeing aircraft and, of course, the automobile manufacturers, and hardly at all for unknown brands and products.

There is a story that should be told (and is, quite often, but not always adequately appreciated) that tells us something about a world where commodity products were replicated and sold simply as manufactured. Here is the product: you should buy it. Back in the aeons of time, when Henry Ford started producing the Model T automobile, his assumption was that mass production would give Ford an edge in pricing over its competitors for what was a commodity product that everyone would want. Black and boxy, read the product description, and Henry Ford was happy until he noticed that his competitors had started making cars that were less boxy and offered variety in the trim, upholstery and other bits. The market was becoming customer-driven, to coin a phrase, and he rapidly responded to the market demand for more individualism or differentiation in his products. Simple observation of modern automobile products shows a staggering array of design, styles, options and prices from manufacturers all over the world, focused on a wide range of customer segments within which each option offered has a market opportunity that can often be defined and targeted. Pushing a product at all segments will probably find a proportion of its actual target buyers but focusing resources on those identified as being within the target segment is likely not only to make the most effective use of available resources, but also increase the probability of gaining sales.

Most markets, domestic and international, are driven by the needs or desires of customers or end-users and the point of a strategy is to position a company so that it can maximize benefit through recognizing and responding most effectively to those expressed desires. In global terms – the world is a large and complex planet – it can generally be argued that in order to achieve this it is necessary to utilize strategies based on priorities so that company resources can be applied to their maximum effect and corporations can gain returns accordingly. The information developed during the course of the WRAP process is used for this purpose, that is, to help prioritize markets and identify opportunities, and strategy evolves as a result of this knowledge and awareness.

Strategic objectives

As discussed in Chapter 5, strategic objectives are initially put in place as a means of providing basic definition and guidance to the WRAP process. It some cases it will be necessary to formulate these objectives without having a sound awareness of their viability. However, as part of the WRAP process strategic objectives can be revisited and changed in the light of information that has been gained during the process. It's a learning curve that adds substantial quality and value to the ambition and viability of the original objectives because they can now be perceived within a wider context encompassing both operational and market considerations.

For example, recall the American firm that sought to duplicate its UK sales in continental Europe. The organization quickly discovered that this new potential market for its products was about eight times as large as the UK market and potential sales simply could not be serviced. The firm's original objectives were shaped by its assumptions, which turned out to be wholly incorrect, about the relative sizes of the UK and continental European markets, and its ambitions were dominated by a desire to increase sales, but only by a little. The company withdrew from this project and returned some years later with a new CEO, a restructured organization and a new set of objectives.

This introduces the issues of time-scale and opportunity. While a firm's long-term vision and ambitions may extend to global sector leadership, the strategies adopted are generally focused on short to medium-term thinking stimulated by the need to provide shareholder value for the current shareholders rather than succeeding generations of fund managers. Although potential futures, defined as 'how should we be positioned in the world in 30 years' time?' are sometimes envisioned by academics and the more esoteric think tanks, such strategic thinking is really in the realm of speculation and, more often than not, optimism. Long-term planning on this scale has been successfully implemented, most notably by the Japanese in the automobile and shipbuilding industries, but it requires an extraordinarily high level of patience, co-operation, focus and dedication that embraces national government, financiers, manufacturers, suppliers and industry workers, which is unlikely to be available to modern enterprises and in any event might well contravene the competition rules of the World Trade Organization.

To be effective, strategic objectives must give corporate direction against which achievement can be measured in some form, and thus their operational time-scale is at its most effective only for as long as the world for which they were devised remains broadly in alignment with the original expectations and forecasts. This assumes that they are established within a sufficient framework of knowledge and understanding of the current international business context. It thus becomes evident that as information gathered during the strategic development process expands the available base of knowledge it will influence thinking about market prospects and development, and the original objectives should become subject to more rigorous review and change as appropriate.

The factors that are most likely to influence change in initial objectives include:-

- Access to more and better information about international markets and their potential in terms of both growth and accessibility
- Increased awareness of internal and external constraints, risks and opportunities
- Increased awareness of corporate strengths and weaknesses in an international context
- Focus on priority targets and concomitant awareness of what these targets offer the organization
- Increased understanding of what may and may not be achievable in terms of both corporate objectives and return on investment

Reaching this level of understanding is often an achievement in itself and represents possibly the most important element in developing and managing strategies whose objectives are not only realistic and measurable, but also offer the immeasurable added value of informed adaptability to changing situations.

Resources and competencies

As Sun Tzu might have said, know your circumstances but above all, know yourself. The over-riding issue for most companies operating internationally is continuing to provide shareholder value while responding to the sometimes complex demands of customers and suppliers who may think differently, speak different languages, work with different currencies and seek to implement their own priorities. A small number of organizations have the size, experience, capacity or will to operate a direct customer interface worldwide, although this does depend to a degree on the industry sector involved, but most will deal with partners, agents, distributors or wholesalers in each country on whom they will be largely dependent for corporate market development.

Dealing with these supply chain organizations tends to take one of two forms: they are managed by the organization, or alternatively they manage the organization. As we have observed previously, the key to control is having access to independent information about local markets and circumstances as well as having the capability to use the information to ensure that an organization's objectives are achieved. This points to a need for strong management and clear direction in international operations of any type: without these there is little likelihood of achieving corporate objectives, and every chance of achieving the objectives of international partners and distributors, which are unlikely to be entirely in alignment with organizational goals. This is a common management and organizational issue, where problems often begin at corporate headquarters as the executive team determines the key principles through which operational activities will be directed, or fail to be directed.

Corporate strengths are sometimes assumed to be equally applicable whether the organization is operating in domestic or international markets, yet these strengths and weaknesses are only relative to the markets or sectors against which they are measured. For example, a company whose mode of international development is focused on acquisition of local firms as the key to market development might find that in some countries, particularly those with a tradition of family ownership or where legal requirements include partnership with local organizations, the acquisition fund simply cannot find suitable targets to acquire. In such cases the strength normally attributed to the fund converts into an irrelevance and if acquisition is a strategic requirement then a number of countries will be excluded from consideration regardless of the business opportunity they may offer. Pricing is another, more common example where a fixed price product may be thought of as competitive in the US, cheap in Europe and expensive in India; the price can be a strength or a weakness depending on the market in which it is offered.

It is vital in any market for a company to exploit its strengths and seek to overcome its weaknesses if it is to achieve success and maximize its potential, and in international business it becomes critical to appreciate that domestic corporate strengths and weaknesses are not necessarily the same thing in the rest of the planet. Figure 9.3 illustrates the divergences that may arise for an imaginary US corporation that is seeking to more fully develop markets already established in Germany and Egypt.

Figure 9.2   Facing up to International Business

A UK firm with a wide product range that was sold in over 70 countries world-wide operated through distributors in each territory, and each product was managed by a brand manager responsible for market development. Domestic sales represented 25 per cent of the global total and the brand managers spent 60 per cent of their time dealing with domestic business. This left just over three months each year when they were available to support and manage the international network which usually involved a short trip to each country, discussion on sales levels and responding to problems with product delivery and technical support. Each year there was a negotiation with each distributor on increasing sales volumes. International communications were maintained by telephone, fax and email and as the brand managers were very busy people these were often handled by secretaries or customer support personnel.

This is a common pattern of international business management and many firms would feel pleased with themselves at creating such a sweetly running operation in which distributors were serviced and visited every year, sales targets were generally and amicably agreed and achieved, predictable returns were made and shareholder risks were minimized. However, any business student should recognize some of the flaws in this operation which became more evident as shifts in global market and economic trends began to create some sales attrition.

International communications with head office in the UK were always poor as command of the English language was not flawlessly uniform throughout the network and neither the secretaries nor the customer support staff in the UK could speak a single foreign language between them. This led to priorities and preferences being given to those distributors whom the staff could easily understand or who were designated as important by the brand managers, while the others were often ignored or left to be handled during the brand managers' annual visit. Supply and support to the domestic market, in any event, took priority over everyone else, and late delivery became the single major complaint around the network. This issue became highly contentious as markets became more competitive, and each sale increased in importance, and it began to seriously affect the brands' competitive edge around the world.

Even more critical was the realization, as the company fought to respond to changing market conditions, that its international sales targets and forecasts were entirely based on those of their distributors and that the company was unable to focus or direct its response to priority markets, as it didn't know which countries these actually were. All it knew were recorded sales volumes and returns, which might bear no relationship to potential sales and market size.

Over the years the corporation had failed to invest in independently researching its markets, in training its staff to respond properly and within priority guidelines to international communications, and in making available sufficient executive time to actually manage the large international network. As a result its strategic objectives were based on feedback from its distributors, each of which had its own business objectives in which sales of the company's products represented only one element in a product portfolio.

And the kick in this company's tail was that its international sales organization comprised brand managers available one day per year per country, with no knowledge of the customers who actually bought the products and no means of measuring distributor performance against market opportunity. The company is now adapting to these revelations and has restructured its international management structure to incorporate regional sales managers whose responsibilities include contact with end users of its products, development of independent market research and improved communication with distributors. The results are not yet known.

Figure 9.3   Divergence in Strengths and Weaknesses

Attribute	US market	German market	Egypt market
Strong US-based management team	Strength	Weakness	Neutral
Strong German or Egypt based management team	Weakness	Strength	Strength
US-based spares service	Strength	Weakness	Weakness
High quality product	Strength	Strength	Strength
High priced product	Weakness	Neutral	Weakness
Known international brand	Strength	Strength	Strength
Known US brand	Strength	Weakness	Weakness
English language customer service	Strength	Weakness	Weakness
Local language customer service	Strength	Strength	Strength
Female management team	Neutral	Neutral	Weakness
Purchase order forms in English	Strength	Weakness	Weakness

It is not suggested that a full SWOT (strengths, weaknesses, opportunities, threats) analysis should be completed for every country in which its products are sold, but at the very least a corporation needs to undertake a substantive review of its international presence as a whole or in a regional context to ensure that potential weaknesses, which may appear as domestic strengths, are either addressed and overcome, or acknowledged to put limitations on the organization's performance. The recognition of relative strengths and weaknesses can also be perceived as important in building strategies targeted at priority regions, countries and sectors where corporations seek not only to enhance their strengths, but also to invest as required to buy the means of sustaining successful competitive strategies.

Many firms fear such change and prefer to take a negative position in addressing markets which they have found difficulty in developing (Figure 9.4). This often takes the form of blaming others when the real problems lie in their own perceptions and lack of awareness, or prejudiced opinion masquerading as objective perception, and there are many examples of entire nations (and major market opportunities) being excluded from strategic consideration for reasons that are really without any solid foundation. For example, there is the saga of the small UK automotive supplier that, through an agent, was given an opportunity to fulfil a major contract for Turin-based Fiat, one of Europe's major auto manufacturers. The firm was shocked to find that the contract documentation was in Italian and that the applicable laws were those of Italy, and refused to respond to the opportunity. Thus it remains a small automotive supplier.

As we discussed in Chapter 8, major limitations on international corporate development are often self imposed, rather than introduced externally, and it is part of the function of management to ensure that international business is approached as professionally as any other part of the company's operations. Strategy provides guidelines on where to go and what is required, yet successful development depends on how the company utilizes its resources to respond to the markets and customers it addresses.

Figure 9.4   We Can't Do Business With Them Because...

1. (UK CEO on France): 'they spend too much time thinking about Napoleon and resent the battle of Waterloo'
2. (German marketing director on the UK): 'we have to understand that they are an island people'
3. (US company owner on Sweden): ' they're not pro-business'
4. (Middle East banker on the US) 'I find it incredible that the American government expects government facilities to compete for its own contracts. Surely it's easier to give them to the best people?'
5. (Japanese trade association executive on the rest of the world): '(silence)'
6. (Egyptian factory executive on European regulatory requirements): 'we prefer to do it the Egyptian way'
7. Newly appointed American international sales executive on the world): 'God, I never knew there were so many countries'

Priority targets

Priority targets are those territories and markets that have been determined as likely to offer the best business opportunity, and they are the places to which the allocation of resources is most likely to yield the greatest benefit. They are not necessarily the only focal point for strategic development, as a strategy must take account of a broader remit in seeking to determine the most appropriate means of achieving corporate objectives, but they do represent the areas that are expected to maximize returns relating to corporate objectives.

At this point in the WRAP process the priority targets will have been selected and subjected to more rigorous examination, probably involving in-country visits to end users, buyers, distributors and other market participants or knowledgeable sources as part of the information development process. The use of this feedback related to corporate resources and ambitions will offer several options for market entry or development. It is also useful to review perceived competitor approaches and strategies both to help identify the market factors that lead to their market positioning, and to determine the nature of the competitive strategies likely to be required in achieving corporate objectives.

For example, in an engineering industry sector review for a European firm, which examined the performance of key competitors in several countries in south east Asia, German companies were found to be the most effective European machinery exporters. One identifiable reason was that in each target territory there was a German technical center that was easily accessible to manufacturers as well as engineering students, and thus local buyers were able to develop familiarity both with the German machines and, to some degree, the German approach to providing them with engineering solutions. The German suppliers provided a high level of customer support and training, which was another factor in their relative success. On the other hand, the next most popular machine suppliers were the Italian firms, although their strength was concentrated in one country and this performance could be traced back to a single distributor. No direct support in the form of training or solutions was provided, Italian representatives were hardly ever seen in the region, yet these firms held a significant share of the imported machinery market.

For the reviewing European firm, the answer to this apparent conundrum was evident. It was much cheaper to find a good distributor who would provide local technical support and thus match the firm's usual mode of international operations. However, the other issues that could have been usefully considered included:-

- *Availability.* How many 'good' distributors existed that were actually available to the company? Furthermore, what characteristics would the distributor need to display in order to be considered 'good'? Were such organizations available in every target territory, or in the region as a whole? The Italian performance was only evident in one target territory, and perhaps they just got lucky in being represented by the best distributor in the entire region.
- *Pricing.* The German machines were more expensive than equivalent technology, yet still held the largest share of the market for European products over the target territories. Was this because buyers were simply willing to pay more for German technology, or because the German investment in the technical centers provided a higher value pay-off?
- *Control and returns.* If it is considered that the priority markets are the most important in the region, offering the most opportunity, then why resource them at the same level and in the same way as non-priority territories, when experience suggests that management by distributor is likely to be patchy and there are no guarantees that

the company's selected distributors will all turn out to be stars? If the German firms increase their returns by putting in appropriate investment, isn't that investment possibly why they hold the largest market share?

There is little point in determining priorities unless they are used to guide investment of one sort or another in the expectation of gaining the maximum benefit from it. Many firms continue to trade in an environment in which the only priority is their domestic market, while other markets which might be expected to provide far greater levels of potential business are treated in the same way, in terms of investment and organization, as much smaller markets. US firms in general, because they are located in the world's largest market for many goods and services, often have relatively low levels of export, yet many of the largest American corporations have grown almost exponentially by addressing world markets. Japan and the major European economies, on the other hand, tend to be more dependent on the profits from international business to finance further investment. This introduces the issue of prioritizing targets since few corporations, even the largest ones, have the either the means or the desire to equally resource all potential national markets.

It is interesting to observe that when a firm's domestic market takes precedence over all others, even bearing in mind that there are good and evident logistical reasons for this, it tends to be treated within annual accounts as separate from international markets. This type of prioritization is usually based on corporate history and development before it became involved in international trade, but it is perfectly feasible in the modern world to view the domestic market as one of many markets and to expect from it a return commensurate with its size. For example, the UK market contains about one per cent of the world's population and because of its relative wealth, perhaps a few per cent of most market sectors. Similar ratios apply to Germany, France, Japan and other countries, yet there is a pervasive urge for most companies to seek to maintain high sales levels in their domestic markets often at the expense of investment in sometimes more profitable foreign markets. This may be attributable not only to simple nationalism and corporate history, but on occasion to the sources of corporate funding themselves, who may insist on immediate dividends at the expense of longer-term strengthening of the global presence.

It can be argued that the opening of many world markets and the development of e-business should stimulate a rethink by many boards of the value that they place on international business in relation to overall corporate profitability and shareholder value, and that perhaps the old adage of maintaining one international executive for every 50 domestic executives should be cast into the recycle bin of history, or simply reversed to take account of international market realities. Risk, of course, must be regarded as an element to be considered, particularly in these troubled times, but it is one of the critical functions of management to minimize and manage risk. Easing the management of risk is one of the reasons why priorities are adopted in addressing international business and this requires appropriate investment in executive time, corporate resources and staff training to maximize the benefit.

In strategic terms, adopting a process of prioritization such as WRAP provides a focus for this investment that ensures reduced risk and greater opportunity and allows strategies to be developed that concentrate effort on gaining or developing the required market positioning both in global terms and in relation to the targets. Luck can sometimes play a part, but as every executive knows, it is not entirely reliable.

Business environment

The business environment can be defined as the way in which business is conducted and the rules, laws, customs and frameworks that regulate this process. Assessing the business environment in any given territory in relation to corporate strategic objectives is an essential part in developing strategies that will succeed; while it is helpful to appreciate local courtesies and lifestyles, the context in which business will be most successfully facilitated is one in which the customers or end-users feel most comfortable. The business environment encompasses local culture, customer behavior, and preferred modes of accessing products or services and dealing with the organizations that supply them, fleshed out with contextual information to provide a more detailed background.

For example, it is important to be aware of customer preferences for supply: that is, whether they prefer to deal direct with manufacturers, with distributors or wholesalers or through retail outlets, mail order, or any other potential route to market. A pragmatic means of identifying a useful route to market may be identified by observing the ways in which competitor's products or services are sold. Objectively there is no reason, of course, why a company should not attempt to distribute its offerings in a novel manner, such as through e-business channels or direct marketing, if these methods are evidently popular in the territories targeted, but if these are new approaches then the risks involved need to be considered. Selecting the wrong delivery mechanism would be a strategic error that would not only increase risk, but also reduce prospects of success.

For example, a small European company that manufactured instrument sterilizers for use in professional medical and dental practices focused on Germany as a priority market and recruited a specialist distributor in the country to market the product. The distributor used a mail order catalogue with a circulation aimed at 50,000 professional offices, and had a solid reputation with both buyers and product suppliers. The company's product comprised an instrument bucket with a sealed lid and was clad in white plastic: it was cheap, effective and reliable.

In the catalogue, however, its picture and those of its competitors sat side by side and a comparison was easily made between the inexpensive plastic bucket and the stainless steel medical instrument container offered by other suppliers. During the two years of its catalogue life not a single sale was made. Three key issues arose:

- *The method of distribution.* It was evident that the target market of professional medical and dental practices generally responded well to the mail order concept. However, a closer examination of their style requirements, possibly extending to office visits, would quickly have identified their preference for equipment that looked and felt both professional and of high quality. This product did not give them these comfort factors and the catalogue pictures simply confirmed their viewpoint.
- *The product.* This was a product new to the German market that sold quite steadily in some other parts of Europe. The assumption was made that Germany would prove to be as receptive to this sterilizer as anywhere else, but no review was undertaken of the workings and motivations of its primary care system, nor of the professional image that German doctors and dentists prefer to project to their patients and, of course, to their paymaster health care insurance organizations. The product in the form it was presented to its potential market proved to be unsuitable; a systematic review of the design of competitive products might well have come up with the simple idea of boxing the bucket in a stainless steel casing.
- *The market priority.* Germany was quite appropriately targeted as Europe's largest health care market, and the primary care segment is

a major feature of this market. But for this product? The company ultimately found a much better target market in supply to the World Health Organization and international charities for use in developing economies where the key product attributes were found extremely useful and style never became an issue.

As in any game, success in international business develops from awareness of the formal and informal rules of play, or the context, as well as the technical skills that are applied. Strategies must take context into account if they are to be successful in providing targets, guidance and methodologies for application by companies in achieving their international objectives. This can be a problem where strategies that are formulaic in approach are implemented in every target territory, as they tend to perform well in countries whose business cultures are broadly compatible with the chosen formulae, and badly in other territories unless suitably adapted.

Context and environment include legal and regulatory issues that can be ascertained through trade bodies, governments and other organizations, although their implications for foreign companies are not always as clear as one might wish. Within the informal structures of many societies, simple compliance with official regulations will prove inadequate in achieving corporate requirements; personal relationships and perceived long-term commitment to a territory are often more important. On the other hand, territories such as the US and those within the EU do demand absolute compliance in bidding for public sector contracts (apart from a favored few exceptions) and will simply bin bids that are evidently non- compliant.

Acting against this spirit was a UK company that over many years failed to win contracts with the US Department of Defense despite of having a strong reputation with the Department as a subcontractor to prime contractors. Eventually a bright spark identified the flaw: the company was bidding in pounds sterling for contracts that, on the front page of each bidding document, stated clearly that all bids should be in US dollars. On being questioned, the bidding manager responsible claimed that he was aware that the United States held substantial funds in British pounds and felt that they should use this money to cover contracts awarded to UK firms. He was unaware that the US was unlikely to change its complex procurement laws, regulations and procedures on his behalf, and thus every bid made was going to be non-compliant on page one unless he could find a way to suppress his feelings and bid in the stated currency.

There is also an informal strand in international business life that could be described as the ability to understand and respond to local issues couched in colloquial language. These are the social factors that come into play during business communications and reflect in some way the credibility, commitment and local awareness of non-domestic suppliers, adding another comfort factor to the contextual framework. This also has a strategic message to be incorporated in the thought process as strategies are developed because its influence can be vital for a foreign company in gaining acceptance as a reliable operation with presence that is likely to continue to exist in the market. It is largely for this reason that firms work with or employ local partners; they have a far better understanding than most outsiders of how their country works and what factors and issues interest and motivate its people. This applies as much in familiar, developed countries as in any other. It is a dangerous assumption that fluency in a local language alone opens the door to commercial riches.

One of the commonest fallacies in the United Kingdom, for example, is that because English is a language that is shared with the United States, the two cultures are also entirely compatible. In the sense that they are both western liberal democracies and have some common values, this is perhaps true, but business relationships are as much influenced by the contextual social factors as any other international relationship. A large UK consulting practice that occasionally worked on US-based projects decided to launch a New York office in order to increase its penetration of this enormous American consultancy market. The firm was based in London and employed large numbers of well-spoken graduates from England's best known universities, many of whom had visited the US on vacation or business. The English accent, they were told, was loved by most Americans and thus it was assumed that this would provide the firm with a unique and popular spin to introduce their consulting services. It took about two years of major investment in premises, accommodation, travel and the salaries and expenses of several extremely upper crust consultants for the practice to realize that while the accent may be loved to death, most Americans actually prefer to buy from Americans.

Business opportunity

In a strategic sense, the business opportunity in a territory or region can be perceived as the strength of the opportunity to enter or develop a market and may comprise either a long term process of gain or a one-off or series of specific identified opportunities to gain business advantage. An opportunity to do business generally exists in most developed economies in most sectors but will generally be available within a highly competitive environment, while in developing economies there are more likely to be some sectors offering high growth and others yet to show significant development.

There are two aspects in particular that require to be considered in reviewing the business opportunity in target markets. The first is the cost-benefit equation, or the level of investment a company is prepared and able to make in order to achieve a preferred or potential return on the opportunity. The second is the nature of that investment. Both involve risk and judgment, even if the company already has assets and operational experience in the target territories. Opportunity has a value and a time-scale that needs to be addressed in relation to corporate management and technical capabilities and there are many options for development within an identified business opportunity that can be considered and compared, depending on the nature and context of the opportunity and the capabilities of the company.

Developing options

Strategy can take many forms and is subject to a wide range of interests invested in its success. Corporate views and requirements for strategy vary from the entirely prescriptive, such as a pre-set formula that requires the use of a distributor, an acquisition format, a sales team, control by a specified manager, or something else, to the derivative based on market-led approaches. The critical issue is to determine which strategic approach is most likely to maximize benefit in terms of strategic objectives, particularly in specific prioritized target territories, which allows a more focused approach to be adopted than might be the case in viewing the entire world or even a single region within it.

It is helpful, before defining the strategies to be implemented, to develop and review key options which provide comparisons in terms of investment and return. These can be devised as a series of matrices or listings to which rankings may be attached, or simply as descriptive scenarios of options judged to be available. If we take a simple example where three options seem feasible for more detailed strategic development, then these can be compared and evaluated using the approach suggested in Figure 9.5 for our old American friends, Smith and Co.

Many tools and matrices have been devised to address this, each with its own presentation and focus, and one we have found to be

Figure 9.5   Reviewing Strategic Options

Background. Smith and Co manufactures a cardiac monitoring device for use at home, serving markets in several European countries as well as the US. Its strategic parameters are focused on western Europe and its priority target markets have been identified as Germany, France, the UK and Italy; the company currently sells products through distributors in the first three territories. Its strategic objective is increased turnover and profitability in European markets.

Options. The company's identified options are:

1. Continue with the current strategy by retaining and supporting existing distributors
2. Create a subsidiary company to closely manage distributor sales in the region, adding Italy to the other territories
3. Create a sales office in each priority territory and sell direct

All other options are excluded for substantive reasons.

Comparative Analysis

Factor	Option 1	Option 2	Option 3
Cost	No extra cost	Annual cost US$250,000	Annual Cost US$1 million
Return	No additional return	Sales increase 50%	Sales increase 200%, management control
Risk	No new risk	Failure by distributors to increase sales to cover new cost	No corporate experience in direct international sales
Objectives	Fails to achieve objective	May achieve objective	May achieve objective

Although the company has been through the WRAP process and developed all the relevant data and information that supports this table, this would still create substantial discussion, probably at its most pungent between the financial officer and the V-P Business Development, because it is the element of risk that is most critical to decisions about to be made, as well as the most difficult to judge. There may be other factors that would influence this decision such as how much money can be made available, the presence or otherwise of another senior executive keen to implement Options 2 or 3, the possible location of the regional office (at which point the presence of golf courses can become inexplicably linked with corporate strategic development), and the company's traditional business style, but in rational terms it is a risk decision for the firm and its shareholders and the results would contribute to the overall performance of the company.

helpful relates corporate competencies to option requirements. In essence, the results show that where corporate competencies are high in relation to the identified strategic options, levels of risk are decreased and the business opportunity enhanced. In the circumstances described in the example above it may be appropriate for the company to initially adopt Option 2, which would provide some experience in international management and limit its risk. Once that experience has been gained in the region, there would be a case for reviewing the options and reconsidering Option 3 as a means of achieving the financial objectives.

This raises the issue of time-scale. In the great wen of events there are always three possibilities. There is now, the present; there is the extreme long term, stretching over decades and centuries; and there is something in between, which companies choose to deal with. The time-scale for implementation of strategies is one aspect of the problem, but the other is the time-scale of payback in reaching the strategic objectives. These need obviously to be linked so that the objectives can be achieved within a reasonably predictable period of time. The determination of options should take this into account as the effectiveness and corporate acceptability of many strategies can be enhanced by targeting development periods to allow for implementation, monitoring and payback, as well as defining the appropriate moments for the extension of a strategic approach throughout a region.

The drawing up of broad scenario statements as an alternative to factor comparison is designed to offer organizations a range of options in which the implications of each option are incorporated as a part of the scenario. Thus whichever option is preferred will carry with it implicit acceptance of the stated implications. Although this approach is highly prescriptive as well as descriptive and tends to lack flexibility in implementation, it does encourage the scenario developers to consider longer term issues, and such scenarios are probably more heavily utilized by governments and public sector organizations than by commercial concerns. The reason for this may lie in the fact that public bodies essentially utilize policies that they hope will achieve desired political, economic or social goals as an explicit or implicit outcome, rather than strategies that can be focused and evaluated in terms of costs, returns and shareholder value.

Strategy development, unless we are dealing in a world of empty markets, also needs to take competition into account. Action tends to generate reaction from domestic and international competitors, and for this reason thoughtful companies seek to develop awareness of the potential moves and motives of their competitors as well as of ongoing market shifts and opportunities. When a number of western health-care disposable manufacturers moved their production operations to Malaysia, Indonesia and Singapore they were chasing not only access to raw materials such as latex, and not only cheap labor rates: they were chasing each other in order to prevent their key competitors from gaining market advantages from lower costs and more dependable material supply. The first company to relocate to the region pursued an aggressive strategy aimed a gaining global market share. As a pioneer, this would have carried a significant degree of risk and cost but would also provide substantial competitive advantage. Later arrivals were pursuing defensive strategies to defend their market share against the lower cost products. Now, the great manufacturing shifts are to China, but the same pattern of action and reaction is evident.

So how much content in a strategy is offensive, and how much defensive? How much should be proactive, and how much reactive? Patently the answers will vary from company to company, sector to sector, and depend on a whole range of competitive circumstances.

On the other side, where a company prefers to apply a prescriptive approach, such as an acquisition policy for both offensive and defensive strategies, the critical issue often comes down to the perceived value of identified acquisition targets in relation to achieving corporate objectives within a timescale that meets corporate requirements. For example, a US healthcare company that sought to achieve European leadership in its sector, simply listed its main competitors and evaluated their potential price and their market penetration so that the acquiring firm needed only to organize the right deal to gain its leadership. However, it quickly became evident that the 'best' targets for acquisition were unavailable and the others were precluded as they did not appear to have the required market penetration, and thus it took several years before the US firm could achieve its objective. This was actually achieved through a combination of small acquisitions and organic competitive growth. It is interesting to reflect that perhaps the acquisition approach was rather too prescriptive in relation to the market sector in which the company operated and focusing on it thus delayed progress being made on the organic growth side of the equation.

Example of a developed strategy

This company is a multi-million dollar corporation based in North America operating in the healthcare sector, and its ambition was to lead the world in its sector. The company had two major competitors and many smaller ones located around the globe and although the single largest market for its products was the US, over 50 per cent of the world market existed elsewhere. It was not fully aware of its global competitive positioning nor of customer trends, but recognized that the changing world of international trade potentially offered a challenge that could be both dangerous and beneficial to its current business. The board determined that a detailed strategy addressing the spectrum of its activities on a worldwide basis was required and took the WRAP route.

Corporate objectives
- Implement a strategy to position the company as world leader in its sector by the year 2000
- Develop global development priorities to support the overall objective
- Address market, competitive and technology issues arising from these developments

Process

Internal Assessment
- Determine current company assets and capabilities in total and by global region. Regions comprise North America, Europe, Japan, Asia, Rest of World

External Information
- Determine market size and trends in total and by global region segmented by applicable technologies (3 applicable technologies)
- Determine current competitive market positioning (against all major competitors) in total and by global region and forecast positioning in 2000 without strategic change
- Determine competitive positioning by applicable technologies

Analysis and Prioritization
- Identify top customer locations, geographic shifts, technology preferences and assess company compatibility
- Identify new potential markets for applicable technologies

Strategic Options: Evaluation and Reassessment
- Determine optional actions in each global region and calculate potential costs and returns

Strategy Development
- Agree on strategy to be adopted

Figure 9.6 shows the development of the company's operating platforms, or centers of activity, from its starting levels (start of strategy development) to the levels achieved by the year 2000 and it can be seen that before taking world leadership there was a game of catch-up to be played with its largest competitor. Although it had a solid platform in Europe which the other key competitors lacked, the information developed showed a major growth trend toward Asia (excluding Japan). The company was also active in only one of three technologies applicable to products in its sector, which meant that only customers with that single preference could consider its products. The strategy deliberately focused on spreading the technology base so that its products could become accessible to all potential customers, but also took account of the company's need to defend its position within its extant technology.

Figure 9.6   Forecast Platforms for Strategy Development

Platform	Company		Competitor 1		Competitor 2	
	Y 1995	Y 2000	Y 1995	Y 2000	Y 1995	Y 2000
Geographic						
N. America	▭	▭	▭	▭	▭	▭
Europe	▭	▭				
Asia	▭		▭		▭	
Japan						
Technology						
Technology 1	▭	▭	▭	▭		
Technology 2	▭	▭	▭	▭	▭	
Technology 3	▭					

The forecast results of the strategy, shown in Figure 9.6, demonstrate the impact and indeed need for this strategy development as forecasts indicated that the corporation's major competitors would increase their market shares over the period. It was therefore essential that the company adopted and implemented its strategy in order to achieve the required market leadership. The costs likely to be involved in this achievement, however, were over US$80 million and this gave the company a new problem.

Figure 9.7 World Competitive Positioning – Starting and Forecast

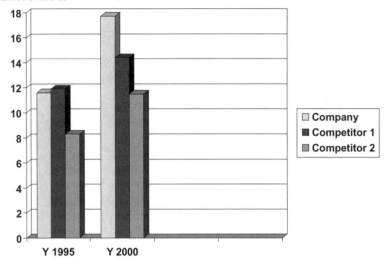

Market Share %

Of course, the next question is, what actually happened? I'll leave the money issue in the air, but suffice it to say that the strategy worked, the company is now effectively dominant throughout its sector, operates in all three technologies and has platforms throughout North America, Europe and Asia in every technology. The effect on the company's competitive position, expressed as market share, is forecast in Figure 9.7; the actual turnout closely reflected the projection.

What to do if it all goes wrong

Events happen. The CEO is replaced by someone who doesn't like the prioritized territories. Company finances are severely damaged by currency fluctuations, or a bad run on the stock market, or a sudden downturn in the sector. Or, as the British people were told during the 1960's by a caring government, 'in the event of nuclear war the banking system may be affected'. What to do?

Patently there are circumstances on which it would be simply foolhardy to attempt to implement a strategy devised for a different situation, and it may depend on a judgment to be made on the potential transience of the change in circumstances to determine how to proceed. Sometimes it is best to put the project on hold, to delay until a more appropriate moment arrives, but a critical consideration must be the timescale in which the strategic objectives require to be attained. Another option is to implement those parts of the strategy that are unaffected by the aforementioned event or circumstance; for example, if only one country in a priority region is affected, then there is no reason to avoid implementing in the others.

The content of the WRAP process, however, provides for retrenchment to an alternative set of priorities for which the strategy can easily be redesigned and although this may not be as effective in meeting the original objectives it still offers the opportunity to maximize the benefit to be potentially gained in the circumstances pertaining at the time. Alternatively, retire to the corner of the room with a bottle of the best Scotch single malt whiskey, or a hubble bubble, or a prayer gong and ponder what might have been.

10

Strategy Implementation and Management

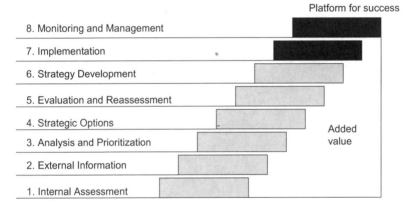

The WRAP Stairway

Platform for success

8. Monitoring and Management

7. Implementation

6. Strategy Development

5. Evaluation and Reassessment

4. Strategic Options

Added value

3. Analysis and Prioritization

2. External Information

1. Internal Assessment

This chapter discusses the importance of rational implementation of the agreed strategy and the added value gained by continuing effective management.

This is the moment, the witching hour, when implementation of the agreed strategy begins and those things that are not known are about to reveal themselves. Many poorly-thought-out strategies fail at precisely this point, when it is discovered that German fire regulations, Japanese working practices, Muslim law, Canadian winters, American distribution channels, Nigerian police, Chinese politics, Russian vodka, Indian poverty, currency exchange rates, medical advances and a revolution in Uzbekistan conspire to deny further market access to the product and thus cause a significant fall in the share price and a rethink both of the strategy and the position of the management team.

Well, perhaps not always so dramatic, but the fact remains that the process of implementation, however carefully thought out, may either uncover or fall prey to unexpected circumstances that throw the strategy off course. In most cases these do not in themselves have catastrophic consequences, but they can operate to divert attention (and often resources) from the achievement of strategic objectives by drawing the organization into a situation of more or less permanent crisis management.

Any strategy that was worth the effort and investment required for development subsequently needs to be actively implemented, and what is implemented requires a degree of deliberate management to ensure that the strategy is operating to meet the objectives and continues to do so over time. It is not unusual for questions of implementation to require some corporate soul-searching, since the achievement of strategic objectives may demand corporate structures and actions with which the organization might be unfamiliar and uncomfortable.

This is also a good time to address another common fallacy of international business: the idea that a well-designed program of implementation will in the long run manage itself. In fact, maintaining a successful global enterprise generally requires significant ongoing investment in time and money. We recall that this was one of the reasons that focus and prioritization were brought into play in the first place. Very few organizations have the resources, or indeed the desire, to give equal weight to every market in which they operate. Therefore, prioritization ultimately functions as a means of allocating scarce resources to the markets in which they can be deployed most effectively to meet corporate objectives. Just as in private life, it may be possible to have it all, but keeping it all demands resources of time, energy, and cash that not everyone can command at all times.

A discussion of the full range of global management and organizational issues is both impossible and out of place in this particular forum. Nevertheless it is appropriate to provide broad guidance on issues of implementing and managing an international strategy. In theory this should be neither more difficult, nor indeed very much different, from implementing a domestic strategy, but as we have seen differences in market conditions, customer preferences, technology requirements, and other variables indicates that the successful international strategy will need to be managed in such a way as to take account of these variables and the way they change over time in different territories.

Components of implementation

In practice, there are four fundamental components for successful implementation of an agreed international business strategy:-

- An action plan that identifies what needs to be done, and who is responsible for doing it
- A broad time-scale for putting this plan into action
- A projected implementation budget
- Plans for longer-term management and monitoring

Action plan and time-scale

An action plan should define those activities that must be fulfiled both in planning and executing the implementation of the strategy. In the first instance it should also identify which person or persons will be responsible for each defined task. The complexity of the action plan patently depends on the strategy or strategies being pursued, and many organizations chart these activities together with the time-frame in which they require to be started and completed, so that everyone involved is aware of the relationships between the tasks and the degree of urgency or priority that needs to be employed.

Time-scales are important as all business opportunity is to some degree time-dependent; international strategy, however, is often predicated on a series of national or regional time-scales that may not operate exactly in alignment with one another. For this reason the capability to reschedule tasks and re-focus initiative within an overall time period becomes critical. Beyond this, there is also the necessity of bringing together different strands of a strategy so that the overall objectives are achieved. These strands can encompass strategic developments in products and services, markets, technologies and location as well as financing, supply chain, distribution and logistics; add to this any necessary recruitment, management activity, communications (internal and external), system change and organizational issues, image change and promotion, all to be undertaken in a range of territories and cultures, and it becomes evident that the planning of implementation can become a major task. Figure 10.1 demonstrates how these strands can feed in to an overall plan.

Timing is an important element in the implementation process. In the global economy it is not always easy to judge the perfect moment to address a given market, as the pace of change and development varies significantly country to country and region to region. The

Figure 10.1 Outline Plan for Strategy Implementation

Function	Preparation	Implement Period 1	Implement Period 2	Implement Period 3
Product, service or technologies	Design	Manufacture or prepare	Supply or apply to priority markets	Supply or apply to secondary markets
Markets	Design systems and communications	Organize supply chain Prepare promotional materials	Launch sales to priority markets	Launch sales to secondary markets
Finance	Fund preparatory work Budget revenue costs Arrange capital routes	Target acquisitions/ partners Negotiate, acquire or contract		
Organization		Recruit and train Integrate systems and communications	Interface with priority markets	Interface with secondary markets

benefit of access to information derived from the WRAP process, including feedback from existing business platforms, comes into play at this stage and should inform the implementation process sufficiently to permit rational judgments on timing to be made. For example, there is a US firm in the healthcare sector whose owner had determined that China should form a part of his company's strategy for global development. He was advised that the timing was wrong for China, which had not at that point reached the levels of market maturity required for successful market development. Unconvinced, he flew to the country to check it out for himself and found that the situation was as described and that his firm should wait a few years before re-addressing this market. But he was not happy as he had set his heart on entering China, and so he acquired a significant share in a noodle factory, and was able to claim early involvement in this fast developing territory. The company followed the time-scale broadly laid out in its strategy and successfully entered the market some years later. Doesn't it seem that the owner showed some wisdom in personally indulging his Chinese passion while allowing his company's strategy, developed at high cost and well informed, to lead his major international business development decisions?

This can work both ways. Sometimes speed is essential in maximizing returns, particularly where the popularity of products or services supplied can vary over time, and it is essential to respond to sudden bursts of buyer enthusiasm by ensuring that the product is actually available for purchase at the point and at the time where demand is highest. Many firms involved in this kind of activity, which includes but is not confined to fast moving consumer goods, take account of this eventuality in their strategies by planning for predictable levels of sales while ensuring that internal or external resources are available for items that become high fliers. In international terms, large firms tend to have strategically located platforms, often subsidiary companies or partners, in various markets available for supply and distribution and sometimes for production, so that priority territories can be serviced quickly. Building and managing these platforms, however, so that they respond as required takes time and early strategic thinking to establish priorities and maintain logistics.

All this argues the need for good planning and efficient implementation, preferably taking only those directly involved and relevant friends and allies into the organization's confidence until the strategy is able to be launched.

Figure 10.2   The Hacienda Built on Sand

A European company in the engineering business followed a strategy that, in part, indicated acquisition of distributors in some key territories. The internal assessment had made it clear that the organization was easily capable of financing such investment, and that the management system already in place could be adjusted to deal with new acquisitions in foreign markets.

Allowing for the usual time-scale of international negotiation, things went well until they reached Spain. Few distributors were available in the country at the price the organizations wanted to pay, and in desperation to meet the demands of the strategy the company started negotiations with its own current distributor, whose organization matched neither the acquisition nor the performance guidelines. Due diligence was undertaken but revealed little. In fact, almost all of the distributor's sales were achieved through a complex network of sub-distributors and agents, almost all of whom had a close personal relationship with the proprietor, and it was unclear how this web of contacts would react to a change of ownership. Nevertheless, the company gulped, then took the irrevocable step of acquiring the distributor's firm at a price of around US$2 million. Within three months the owner had disappeared into the sierras, his network fell out of communication, and the company was left with a name.

Rather than search for another distributor at that point, the company decided that some strategic deviation was required and recruited a well qualified Spanish manager to build a new network. In effect, it replaced one quite well established distributor with an unknown person and was attempting to build the business from scratch all over again. Courage, mon brave!

In this instance, the acquisition strategy was not in itself the cause of the organization's difficulties in this territory. The investment of a little more patience in identifying an appropriate acquisition, coupled with a little more cash, might have offered a more effective route to implementation of the strategy. The company did have more money available and was capable of making more time in the cause of getting it right, but impatience combined with reluctance to pay the going rate for a sound acquisition has made a long-term dent in their performance in the territory.

Implementation budgets

As any financial officer knows, doing anything costs money, and simple speculation seldom leads to accumulation on anything like the scale preferred. But investment in implementing a strategy that is information-based and risk-assessed should deliver the expected benefits and move the organization closer to achieving its overall corporate objectives. If the strategy is worthy of implementation, then the costs of that implementation need to be calculated and made available.

Budgeting for strategy implementation is essentially similar to planning expenditure for established management functions. The additional expenditure anticipated during the implementation phase can in most cases be itemized and planned within the implementation program. Possible exceptions are the potential costs of acquisitions, greenfield investments, investment in joint ventures or other major items that are not fully definable at this early stage. Decisions about undertaking this type of investment may well be taken separately, after implementation is underway. Nevertheless, the initial internal assessment will have provided a broad idea of how much money is available for such investment, and this figure should be taken into account in working out the putative implementation budget.

Much of the cost of developing and implementing a strategy is loaded into the early stages of the process, when investment in management time and travel expenses accrues rapidly. With this in mind, beware the sad tale of the small UK IT system developer that reviewed its strategy and determined its international target markets to be in south and east Asia. After the company's first trips to the area had identified its first potential customer, a large industrial group, and taken this customer to the point of buying its system, the finance director advised the board that, in his opinion, too much money had already been spent with no discernable outcome. Consequently, he recommended that no further funds be made available for this development. The project was dropped and the US$40,000 sunk into the project was effectively lost. So was the customer prospect, and so was its first international venture, principally because no one had made any internal assessment of finance available in the first place.

Project management or facilitation

No matter the size and complexity of the strategy being implemented someone in the organization, in most cases the CEO, must hold ultimate responsibility for its successful completion so that delays can be minimized by accessing his or her decision-making authority if unexpected circumstances occur. Managing international implementation can swallow large amounts of time, and although even busy managers can usually take on some aspects of the additional effort required in each of their areas it can be difficult to maintain equilibrium and momentum throughout the implementation process. This argues the case for a project manager or team charged with monitoring progress and ensuring that the action plan, including all aspects of the strategy, is achieved.

Corporate development, particularly in dealings with partners external to the organization, demands both executive authority and negotiating skills to ensure that the actions required to meet the strategic objectives are activated in the best and most effective manner. In many countries where personal relationships are highly rated it is an expectation that change will be personally directed by the company's chief executive or, at the very least, by known senior personnel. These relationships are often of sufficient importance to the successful implementation of the strategy that it is well worth responding as required. In these circumstances, much of the work of organization and co-ordination can nevertheless be successfully carried out by an appointed team or project manager.

Consultants can also be useful in this task, particularly if the consulting firm has been involved in the development of the strategy. The background knowledge gained during the course of the strategy development program and their awareness of the thinking behind the final strategic recommendations may be valuable in persuading the less well informed of the merits of the strategy. Some companies use a mixed team of executives and consultants to implement more complex strategies, while others utilize consulting services purely as facilitators, to keep everyone's eye on the ball and to help ease more difficult situations.

There are, of course, companies that do none of these things and simply drive new strategies through in the same way as they operate their day-to-day activities. It should be said that firms that use deliberate international strategy development programs such as WRAP gain significant added value from the information gathered and issues considered during the process. This information has practical value not only in prioritization and strategy development; it can also be brought into play to ensure that implementation is achieved as speedily and effectively as possible. Those without the benefit of this awareness and information may also find it more difficult to understand and counteract the multitude of problems and issues that can arise during implementation. This situation becomes a particular problem when international strategies are determined at headquarters in one country, and rolled out without further consideration to the rest of the world.

For example, a large American corporation in the manufacturing sector determined that its sales function in the US, handled through a network of independent distributors, would in future be brought in-house. This is a major decision that involves considerations of staffing, premises, technical support, cash flow and corporate image. A direct sales team for the US market was recruited, trained and put to work, and the 'rest of the world', which represented over 60 per cent of the company's product sales, was directed to do likewise. As the ripples spread, the difficulties increased. The strategy worked well in the UK and Germany, where the corporation already had offices, but in most countries there were no corporate offices and therefore no premises in which either to demonstrate the products or locate a sales team. As the effect of the edict spread from west to east, it finally reached south east Asia where it became immediately evident that most competent and trained technical sales personnel already worked for local distributors and were not about to take what was, for them, the highly risky step of joining a foreign company that might dispense with their services in short order if it changed its strategic thinking.

During this process, of course, the distributor network became steadily more de-motivated. As luck would have it, the current recessionary cycle simultaneously reached its lowest point. Sales dipped all round the world, but the decline became more evident the further the market was from the US; international market shares tumbled, as did the share value of the corporation. It was one of the company's European offices that held responsibility for 'rest of the world' sales, and it was there that the purge of marketing personnel was carried out, from the global sales manager downwards. What happened next? We'll have to wait and see, but perhaps there is a sinking feeling that US headquarters might make another strategic decision.

Managing the strategy

When the strategy is implemented and working according to plan to achieve the designated objectives, all seems right with the world. The organization's (naturally) efficient day-to-day management structure reassumes its role, and the corporate strategists can go home to rest for the next few years. But the perception that a strategy is 'working well' doesn't mean that business will take care of itself. During the strategy development process, strategic objectives are likely to have changed significantly, and the organization may well have undergone substantial change along with them. If the implemented strategy isn't actively managed it is likely to suffer what we call 'strategy drift:' in which the organization's carefully-defined objectives become obscured by day-to-day problems and lose significance, and the company gradually loses it focus on what it is trying to achieve and why.

Over a period of years this situation is probably inevitable as the firm seeks to address new challenges within an ageing strategy and adapts itself on a piecemeal basis to changes in the global market and corporate fortunes. People and technologies move on, competitors adopt more effective responses, stock markets fall and rise and any number of events and circumstances occur to alter the premises on which the strategy was originally based. This argues the case for occasional strategy audits and adjustments to help ensure that the company maintains its focus until, ultimately, it can refocus its energies on a new strategy.

Premature strategy drift, however, tends to occur soon after the implementation team finishes its endeavors and hands over to local management. Its detectable symptoms include highly variable performance and achievement between territories relative to targeted performance, substantial failures in communication and support between head office and territorial activities, elements of vagueness or inaccuracy in international management reports and limited evidence of performance movement toward the achievement of stated strategic objectives. These symptoms are quite common in international business, and in the eyes of many firms they may appear to be simply a part of normal management operations and therefore undetectable as an incipient malaise. Although companies tend to have a pretty good idea of what performance can be expected in their domestic markets, similar awareness in foreign or international markets is much rarer.

The added value offered by WRAP and similar processes can be applied to identify and alleviate these symptoms because the information and analyses generated during the strategy development program also provide an opportunity to monitor the continuing effectiveness of the strategy, provided that simple updating actions are taken at regular intervals. This may, for example, encompass an annual review of readily available data, supplemented by more focused research and analysis on a biannual basis or as profound and highly visible alternations in the market environment demand more up-to-date information. Corporate performance monitoring is a familiar element in company management, or should be, and it requires little additional effort to ensure that progress toward the strategy is maintained and achieved at the pace required.

There are many ways in which the WRAP process can be used as a continuing management tool for ensuring that the full benefits of the agreed international strategy are achieved. The process itself creates the measures by which monitoring can be activated as the strategy settles into its routines after implementation. These are described at Figure 10.3.

A key element in the management of strategy that gets little attention in the literature is the basic drive and doggedness that is required to ensure that the strategy is in fact properly implemented over the required timescale in the face of the many intervening factors that are likely to be encountered. In a company's domestic environment it

Figure 10.3   Using the WRAP Process for Managing Strategy

WRAP process element	Purpose	Potential use in strategy management
Internal assessment	Determines corporate ambitions, culture, strengths, weaknesses	Monitor operating effects of organizational change
External information	Provides independent market information and data	Update regularly to monitor international market performance
Analysis and ses prioritization	Prioritizes targets	Use information analy- to inform company on performance in priority targets and any changes in priorities
Strategic objectives	Desired outcome of strategy	Measure progress towards achievement
Strategy	Means of achieving strategic objectives	Check that strategy guidelines are applied in all relevant places and take remedial action if required

tends to be easier, although not necessarily simple, to work with or put together a team with reasonable commonality of culture and awareness that is capable of ensuring that appropriate action is taken. The finance director deals with the financial strategy, the manufacturing director puts the required processes into place, the marketing director draws up the promotional plans and sorts out the distribution chain, the human resource staff recruit additional expertise or bodies as required, and the CEO leads and manages the process while his or her chairman ensures that the board is supportive. All the other partners – banks, accountants, lawyers, advertising agencies, service suppliers, and others – in modern business are kept informed as appropriate and the whole implementation process works smoothly and successfully. Almost.

Although the principles are the same, the timescale and logistics of implementing international strategies often require a great deal of patience to be added to the mix of drivers. Communications are more difficult particularly where the nuances of technical or strategic innovations and change need to be explained to overseas managers or distributors, and it is often preferable to provide printed instructions and explanations that can be followed up for more detailed discussion.

Acquisitions, joint ventures and partnerships will take considerable time to negotiate, not because they are intrinsically more complex than domestic acquisitions but because contracts and documentation will probably require to be provided in at least two languages and the involvement of two or more legal systems will inevitably require the intervention of an equivalent number of sets of lawyers. Nevertheless a well-founded and properly resourced strategy should provide sufficient guidance to permit its implementation and management in the most effective manner available. A successful international strategy requires not only the application of intelligence and sensibility to recognize different circumstances but also the physical and mental energy to respond appropriately to them.

Conclusions

In a world that is rife with management tomes, business advice, and global gurus, issues of international business and global strategic development are often treated as an adjunct to wider matters of corporate management and organization. In truth, as the practicing international manager or strategist will know from experience, global business carries particular challenges and complexities that benefit from being specifically addressed in a knowledgeable manner. The world is wide, within it the possibilities for action are almost endless, and sound information about those possibilities is often in short supply. How then is it possible in practice to make rational decisions about where and how to commit resources globally?

This issue is becoming more pertinent to businesses of all types and sizes as the developed world learns that globalization is not just something that affects poor peasants far away. The global flow of goods and services is impacting on the ability of many organizations to compete and maintain margins in their domestic market, thus depriving them of further opportunity for complacency. Never mind the mountain coming to Mohammed: organizations that fail or refuse to recognize and address the challenges of operating in a global business environment are likely to find that environment enveloping them even as they relax in the comfortable familiarity of the home market. It's rather like the challenges posed by global warming. Even those who do not contribute to the problem, or indeed those who prefer to believe it doesn't exist at all, will eventually find it necessary to cope with and manage the difficulties created by changes that may be poorly understood yet carry global effects.

The WRAP process was devised as a practical and flexible tool for coming to grips with the challenges inherent in developing rational global operations. This process operates through taking account of the organization's internal resources and capabilities, as well as an assessment of the external environment in which the organization needs or desires to operate, and strikes a balance between the two in order to position the organization successfully in the global marketplace. The process can be used in its entirety as a means of working through issues pertaining to global strategy development; equally, WRAP may be broken into modules capable of addressing specific strategic issues, or as a contribution to the management and monitoring of an implemented strategy.

The power of WRAP is essentially derived from two aspects of the process. Its guides the strategist through a range of thought processes pertaining to various facets of international business activity, facilitating consideration of the opportunities and challenges that arise and operating to place these in a wider context. WRAP also facilitates the prioritization of objectives and opportunities, ensuring a level of focus that permits the organization to more objectively plan investment and return in international markets. This in turn allows the strategist to identify and assess the risks inherent in any global development and permits a more rational allocation of corporate resources on a global basis, deploying them where they can be used most effectively.

Finally, WRAP can be utilized as a framework for implementation and management of a global strategy, a sorely neglected topic in the annals of international management. The process adds value at this stage by providing a basis of information that supports longer-term management and monitoring, and which can be easily updated or expanded as the need arises.

The foundation of the WRAP process is one of constructive engagement with the global environment. As the reader will remember from Chapter 1, constructive engagement requires information, the use of judgment, and a willingness to think outside the boundaries of the individual's own cultural, social, and professional experience. This way of thinking and working offers a more rational and less emotive approach to dealing with the world. Such an approach is now essential, and not only for business reasons.

Figure 10.4   Five Golden Rules of Global Strategy

1. *Know the organization's capabilities and limitations.* Since it's necessary to live and work with them, be aware of their existence and how they can be adapted to meet new challenges in global markets.

2. *Remain focused on strategic objectives.* These objectives exist in order to inform and guide both strategy development and day-to-day management. Keeping them actively in mind reduces the risk of falling into a permanent state of crisis management and prevents strategy drift.

3. *Prioritize.* Just as there is never enough time in the day, there are never enough resources to fulfil all the needs and desires of any organization. Find out where these resources can best be applied and focus on using them in that way.

4. *Believe that information is power.* No, it's not just a slogan popularized by another generation; it's the only means of becoming oriented in a world that is large, diverse, and mostly very, very unfamiliar. Information empowers not just by providing knowledge, but by providing the impetus to recognize ignorance and remedy it through enquiry.

5. *Cultivate flexibility.* This means both flexibility towards unfamiliar circumstances and situations, and flexibility towards the organization itself. Just as it is counterproductive to try to force foreign partners or customers to conform to a preconceived pattern of behavior, it is unproductive to demand that the organization resource activities that will bring it little discernable benefit.

Bibliography

Ansoff, Igor. *Corporate Strategy*. Harmondsworth: Penguin Books, 1988.
Drucker, Peter F. *The Practice of Management*. London: Pan Books Ltd., 1958.
Gannon, Martin J. *Understanding Global Cultures*. Thousand Oaks: Sage, 2001.
Geertz, Clifford. *The Interpretation of Cultures*. London: Fontana, 1993.
Johansson, Johny K. *Global Marketing: Foreign Entry, Local Marketing, and Global Marketing*. McGraw-Hill Higher Education, 2000.
Mintzberg, Henry, Bruce Ahlstrand, Joseph Lampel. *Strategy Safari*. London: FT Prentice Hall, 1998.
Pinker, Steven. *The Blank Slate*. Harmondsworth: Penguin, 2002.
Sun Tzu. *The Art of War*. Oxford: OUP, 1963.
Trompenaars, Fons. *Did the Pedestrian Die?* Oxford: Capstone, 2003.

Index